T5-AFF-070

Prisoner of Innocence

Prisoner of Innocence

Donna Montegna

Launch Press

Walnut Creek, California

© 1989 by Donna Montegna.

All rights reserved. No part of this book may be reproduced or transmitted in any form or by any means, electronic or mechanical, including photocopy, recording or any information storage or retrieval system, without written permission from the publisher.

Printed in the United States of America

97 96 95 94 93 92 91 90 89   5 4 3 2 1

Library of Congress Cataloging in Publication Data

Montegna, Donna, 1952 –
Prisoner of Innocence / by Donna Montegna
p.   cm.

ISBN 0-9613205-7-5   : $8.95

1. Child molesting—United States—Case Studies.   2. Grandparent and child—United States—Case Suudies.   3. Incest—United States—Case studies. I. Title.

HQ72.U53M66   1989
        306.877′092—dc20   89- 12775

                                                    CIP

To my daughter, Candice, the light of my life, who taught me what it means to love.

To Sally Stevens, ACSW. Whose love and support made this dream a reality.

To Debra Smith, LCSW. Who helped me find the courage to look beyond the pain.

Acknowledgements

For their constant support, editing and much more, my deepest appreciation to Constance Gilpin, Marci Siegel, Eunice Jacobson, Lois Berensen and Elaine Marks.

Lush white flakes collect on the window sill. I sit here feeling the dark warmth of the dog's fur beneath my fingers. The peace of this solitary winter afternoon is pierced by the shrill ringing of the telephone. Reluctance to abandon the quiet of the moment is evidenced in the heaviness of my steps to the kitchen telephone.

"Hello", a voice from the past catches me off guard. "I'm real good, how about you?"

The beat of my heart increases, fear and excitement indistinguishable. It's been so long since I've heard my eldest brother's voice. My mind wanders to other times, other places, as he mutters superficially about the boredom and frustration of his daily life. Jimmy, my childhood hero, my idealistic fantasy of the type of man I would grow up to marry. I remember his smile with fond warmth, the way it seemed to sneak out sideways before bursting into it's full radiance, lighting up his boyish face. I try to imagine him in his youthful splendor. The hushed tone of his loneliness won't allow such illusion.

"I know, I guess I never thought things would be like they have turned out to be either. I certainly didn't see myself living like I do. I thought I'd grow up, get married and have lots of kids running around."

I tried to see Jimmy as he sounds today, graying and desperate for another shot at the rainbow and am confronted with my own need to deny his pain. Jimmy rambles on, hesitantly saying too many words I don't want, can't bear to hear. His words echo across the miles filling me with sadness and a burning shame. I struggle with my conflict, knowing I should feel rage or at the least anger in response to his self proclaimed kinship with our grandfather. Yet all I can muster forth is a slight tinge of disgust, unfortunately, yet naturally, directed at myself.

"Well, I have to go, we're on our way out." I struggle to keep the panic from my voice. "Yeah, make sure and send everyone my love. Bye Jimmy, take good care of yourself." Slowly placing the telephone in its cradle, battling to break the unwelcome connection with my past. I lean against the wall stunned by my loss of control.

Mother is standing in the doorway, her arms braced against the frame. Her face is a distorted mask of anguish, her brown eyes clouded over as if to shield her from what she cannot allow herself to see. The weight of grandpa's body crushes my own, smothering the air from my lungs. His knees stretch mine apart viciously. His breath is hot and foul against my neck. Mother is frozen in the entryway, her nails digging into the wood, her chest heaving as she gasps for breath.

"Mama! Mama! Mama help me!" Tears flood my contorted face. Mama doesn't seem to hear my hysterical pleas, she stares past me as if entangled in a nightmare she knows must not be real. My cries shatter the deafening stillness of the encapsulated moment. "Mama! Mama! Please Mama!" I'm beating him with flailing, powerless hands. My throat clenches around useless cries for rescue while moans of terror and suffering are all that escape.

Grandpa, turning his head towards the door, sees his daughter and releases me from his violence. Mother is screaming, a wild primitive and mournful wail from deep within. Grandpa rushes to her, hastily pulling up his trousers as he rationalizes the rape of her youngest child.

"It isn't what you think Suzzanne, really. Oh Jesus Suzzanne! Listen to me God Dammit! I was just trying to teach her something. Suzzanne, are you listening to me? Suzzanne, please!"

His lies stumble from his gaping mouth and soar past her. Mother runs from the room, her agonized moans fill my ears, drowning out the demands of her father's deceit.

Moving day was the ultimate fun and excitement for me. By the time the moving men arrived with our belongings my mother could hardly contain my boundless energy.

"Go on outside and play now Jen. You've been complaining for months about how much you miss your little friends so go on out there and play. Go on girl, get out of this mess and go have some fun."

"Aw mama, everyone's at school, can't I help you unpack and stuff?"

Mama's scowled expression quickly became a grin as she kissed the top of my ruffled hair. She pushed me gently out the door and scurried back to the mayhem of our new home on Columbus Avenue. As I stepped out onto the street where I had spent the first five years of my life I felt like I was really home. The past year, living in the country, had been like visiting a foreign land. No matter how hard I tried, I felt like I could never quite fit in. Everything seemed so different in Stoney Brook, its barren snow covered hills and small town atmosphere greatly contrasted with this city of overcrowded rowhouses and small streets teeming with multicolored people. Our family had changed in that one short year. Mama had married Peter, expecting him to replace my daddy who had died when I was a baby. I didn't want him for a father now or then. I was relieved that he wouldn't be living with us any longer.

But it wasn't only having Peter around that made us all so different, it was much more. Before the fighting began, we used to laugh a lot. Now it seems as though nothing is very funny. Playing with Jimmy was the best part of living in the big old farm house. My big brother is so big and strong and so much fun. The sound of our laughter would fill the air when he took me flying down the icy slopes on his back. Even Debbie has changed. My once smiling sister has been replaced by a scowling and resentful teenager. Maybe things will be better now that we're home and Peter is gone. Home, Columbus Avenue is home. At least it used to be before we had to move to the big farm house where everyone screamed at each other. I'm glad to be back here, maybe now we'll be happy again.

I sit on the curb, dangling my scuffed sneakers in the gutter and play toe tag with Baby Ruth wrappers and cigarette butts. Old Columbus Avenue memories of stickball games and snow forts rush over me as I search the windows above for a familiar face. With everyone either at work or at school, the street seems strangely silent. I walk up one side of the short street, playing a solitary game of kickball with a cobblestone from the road. The YMCA where my friends and I used to ring the bell and run before anyone could answer is still here. On the opposite corner stands the police station where we sold lemonade to the officers in the sweltering heat of summer in the city. Crossing over, I discover that someone has planted a garden where one of our clubhouses used to stand.

Skipping down the sidewalk, I feel free and happy to be home where everything is safe, and people don't yell all the time. The sight of old Mr. Goldfarb standing in the doorway of his flower shop brings a smile to my face as he asks me where I've been keeping myself. Walking and staring at everything, yet I can't quite believe that any of this is real. I run my fingers along the rough brick houses as I round the corner and head back home. Such a wonderful neighborhood of tall buildings with black fire escapes where flower pots and old towels soak up the late afternoon sun. Chinese laundries and corner markets are everywhere, providing a special treat for the kids sent to drop off a soiled shirt or buy a loaf of bread. So much noise, horns honking, cats screeching wildly, old ladies rummaging through trash cans, and people calling out to each other across their alley windows. So different from the country house where the only sounds I was sure to hear were mama and Peter fighting. The city sounds unusually safe after the oppressive silences and threatening rumbles of my country home.

Running carelessly up the steps of our new house I find the place in total chaos. People everywhere, moving this, carrying that. Furniture standing on end and boxes stacked to the ceiling. I try to sneak past mama and climb the stairs to my new room.

"Well there's my girl! Come here sweetheart, give grandpa a big kiss!" I run quickly and jump up into Grandpa John's big arms. It feels so good to be with my favorite grandpa again, his arms feel warm and strong as I snuggle contentedly. "Want to play with me grandpa? We can play hide and go seek or something, you wanna?"

Grandpa readily agrees and we go into the living room in search of places to hide. He is the seeker and I get to discover the most secretive places in which to squeeze my thin body and hide. Every time he finds me he lifts me up high above his head and wraps his long arms around me tightly. I am hiding between two overstuffed chairs, bending over frontwards, my short dress bunched up over my lower back. Large roughened hands are rubbing my bottom briskly I turn, startled, to find grandpa John smiling at me. Laughingly, I run off in search of another hiding spot, grandpa chases me as if playing tag, I run giggling all over the room, over the couch and under the dining room table. Grandpa is holding me close to his chest, the scent of his aftershave strong and pungent his hands playfully caressing my bottom.

"My sweet Jenny, you're so warm and soft. I'm so glad you're going to be living right down the street from grandma and me. We're going to spend a lot of time playing together, okay Jenny?"

"Sure grandpa, that'll be fun."

I'm off again in search of the perfect hiding place. Grandpa is pretending he can't find me, hemming and hawing until grabbing me tenderly from behind the television set. We laugh and hug each other tightly.

"Jenny, what in the world are you doing in here?" Mama's voice is playful yet insistent, "Go on outside girl, you're just in the way, now get out of here!"

"Oh mama, grandpa and me are having fun, can't we play just a little longer, please?"

"No Jenny, not now, you'll have lots of time to spend with grandpa. Right now I need his help so you get outside and don't come back until I call you."

I think the sun rises and sets on mama. Even though her tiny brown eyes are cloudy and too deeply set to be pretty and her large protruding teeth dominate her thin face I think she is the most beautiful woman alive. Mama says she is just plain Jane but that once she felt beautiful. She said my daddy thought she was beautiful so she believed him. Mama dreamt of being a famous movie star when she was a kid like me. Someday maybe I will become famous and mama will be proud of me. I collect pictures of movies stars in a big cloth scrapbook just like she did when she was little. Mama still likes to go to the movies, she says they are the perfect escape. Mama fell in love with my daddy when she was just fifteen and when he died eleven years later she says a part of her died too. I don't know about things like that, she looks all alive to me though she does look sad a lot of the time.

Mama works so hard to take care of us four demanding children. She is tired most of the time. She not only holds down a full time job uptown but she works evenings in her parent's dark room. Mama is proud of her skills as a photographic lab technician and says it's the only thing she does well, but I tell her she's the best mama in the whole world. She just chuckles a little and changes the subject. I've always wanted Mama to teach me how to make the beautiful pictures from the thin black strips of negatives like her daddy taught her. Sometimes she lets me watch her make miracles in grandpa's basement darkroom but she says she's much too busy to teach me how to do it by myself. It seems that being responsible for us kids is just too much for her, she just doesn't seem to have the strength to really be there with us. Mama says she probably should have had just one kid. I wonder which one she'd choose, probably not me since I'm the last one.

When Jimmy was born mama was only sixteen but she and daddy were so happy to have a son. She tells everyone that Jimmy was the most beautiful baby she had ever seen. Jimmy is still devilishly handsome. He is also my favorite brother and someday I'm going to marry a man that looks just like him. He has dark, curly hair that he combs for hours in front of the hall mirror. He loves Elvis and seems to think he is the spitting image of the famous star. He has the most wonderful smile, the kind that seems to sneak out sideways before bursting into its full radiance and lighting up his entire face. His eyes are bright and clear and seem to twinkle with secrets all his own. He doesn't talk a whole lot but seems to communicate plenty with his dancing face. When he does talk his voice is low and gentle and his words come out slow and easy. He has become a real ladies man and has lots of girlfriends" I like to sneak behind the living room door and watch him kiss and hug until he discovers me snooping and sends me outside with a quarter to buy candy. Jimmy and David spend a lot of time together but I have no idea why, they seem so different from each other.

David and I don't get along at all. I don't think he likes me any better than I like him. He says I'm a pest. He is the total opposite of my idol Jimmy. David is tall and straight, lifeless really, as if he were being propped up from behind. His black hair is dull and lifeless and is cut close to his head in the style that was, popular when he was much younger. His eyes are large and dark yet they seem opaque and cold. He is the kind of person that gives no hint as to his feelings or thoughts, kind of like a large brick wall that someone has scribbled on. He doesn't say a lot either but when he does his voice has an icy chill to it. The best thing about David are his teeth, they are perfectly white and straight, and sort of glow in the dark. He is the only one of us with nice teeth. I do envy him that, but nothing else. My own teeth are much too large for my mouth and I can never close my lips over them. David is keenly intelligent, mama says, but things sure seem difficult for him. Especially when he is forced to compete with his charming older brother. He doesn't cause mama the problems that Jimmy does though, he just goes about his life not involving anyone else. When mama does get angry with him it usually has something to do with Jimmy too. David and I rarely talk to each other, we simply have nothing in common. It seems that even though we share the same mother we are not brother and sister, not where it counts anyway. I tend to avoid David. Sometimes I think there is a time bomb buried deep within him just waiting for the right moment to explode into a million fragments. I sure don't want to be around when it goes off. He kind of scares me though I don't fully understand why. He gets along the best with Debbie. They appear to share the same secret, my hunch is that they both hate mama.

Debbie was supposed to be mama and daddy's last child, the girl they had dreamed of. She is my big sister and I work hard at loving her. I always want her to act like the big sisters on television but somehow things never turn out that well for us. I think Debbie hates me, she sure acts like she does. She yells at me a lot, she says it's my fault that mama makes her take care of me and that I should never have been born. Maybe she's right, if I weren't around then she could be with her friends like she wants to be. Maybe then she wouldn't have that face with a frozen sullen sneer. Debbie is heavy, the kind that grownups used to call baby fat and think was cute, now she has become another fat adolescent and she hates everyone because of it, including herself, maybe herself most of all. Her large brown eyes are hidden, as if by design, behind a messy frame of dark frizzy hair that she can never quite fix the way she wants to. Her chubby cheeks are scarred with pimples that she attempts to hide with mama's makeup. Debbie scares me too but I feel sorry for her, she always looks so sad and angry at the same time. I want to love Debbie. She is my big sister. I just wish she'd act more like Mary on the Donna Reed show.

I am mama and daddy's last child, the only one they never thought about having. I was born in the Spring of '52 when Daddy first became seriously ill. I was christened Jennifer Marie because daddy thought the name sounded like someone who would be rich and famous. Someday I hope to be rich at least, I don't think I'd like being famous, too many people would want to talk to me and I wouldn't like that. When mama discovered she was pregnant she didn't know what to do. Daddy was too sick to work so she had to. Somehow it all worked out because here I am. Mama says I cried a lot when I was a baby and that daddy was the only one that could comfort me. I wish daddy were here now. Everyone else remembers him except me. He died when I was only eighteen months old.

People tell me I'm pretty but I don't think so. My hair is light brown, unlike anyone else, and it's the kind that mats into painful snarls not matter how often it is brushed. Mama says a woman's hair is her crowning glory but I think mine is just a bother. I have green eyes, again the only ones in the family. Mama says they're so clear that it's like looking into a pool of crystal water. I just think they are different from everyone elses. Debbie told me that I don't look like anyone else in the family because I was adopted but mama got mad at her and said she was just teasing me. I don't know, maybe mama doesn't want to tell me the truth. No ne is as skinny as I am either even though I can eat almost as much as Jimmy. David calls me stringbean and Jimmy calls me a carpenter's dream, whatever that means. Mama says I'm accident prone. I fall down a lot and always have scrapes and bruises on my knees and elbows, but don't most little kids? She also tells me I'm smart. She thinks I should be a doctor when I grow up but I don't want to. I hate blood so I think I'll be a teacher instead. Everyone has something to say to or about me, most of which I don't like.

Settling into life on Columbus Avenue was easy and fun. Mama enrolled me in the first grade after taking me uptown to buy three pretty new dresses and a pair of new shoes. I thought school was wonderful and imagined myself to be teacher's pet. I believed I was the smartest person in the class, if not the whole world. I was proud of my scholastic achievements and received much attention from mama because of them.

The walk to and from school was almost as much fun as being in class. My neighborhood friends and I would race the three blocks, kicking trash in the gutters along the way. The school-yard was always vibrantly alive with the sounds of screaming children all trying to be heard at once. I quickly established myself as a leader among my peers. I also worked diligently at my lessons, trying to learn all there was to know. My passion for discovering new things seemed boundless. Since I usually finished my assignments ahead of time, Miss Stevens would reward me by letting me erase the blackboard and run errands for her. Miss Stevens was the perfect teacher, just like the ones I'd seen in old movies on television. She was absolutely beautiful, with blonde hair tucked neatly into a soft bun and big blue eyes that seemed to have a life all their own. Whenever she walked by, I would inhale her sweet perfume deep into my lungs until I felt I would burst with her deliciousness.

The move back to the East Side was all and more than I had hoped it would be. Our house was great, there were three flights of stairs to run up and down. I even had my own room for the first time ever. I had hated sharing a room with Debbie, she was too messy for my compulsively neat nature. I was involved with all my old friends again and nearer to my grandparents who I had missed during our time in Stoney Brook. At home life was fairly routine. Between school, playing outside, attending church three times a week and family gatherings we were kept busy. Mama was working long hours trying to support us and we didn't see much of her. I never seemed able to spend all the time that I wanted with her. Even when mama wasn't working she was often away from home. She appeared to be caught up with either church or family matters that required her to be gone frequently. She depended on her parents for nurturance and guidance so she spent what little free time she had talking around Grandma Sarah's kitchen table. Mama didn't have many close friends, so she used her parents to fill the social gaps in her life.

Since Peter and mother had separated we saw him infrequently, which was fine with me. I had never liked Peter. The first time mama brought him home for dinner I thought he was real creepy. He was too old, bald, and as skinny as a ravaged skeleton. He looked much more like a grandfather than the handsome father I had envisioned for myself. Mama tried to make me call him daddy but I refused, there were lots of fights about this issue when we had lived in the country. Peter was just a pesky old guy who chained smoked cigarettes. His smoke always got in my eyes and made them burn. He used to swear a lot too which was forbidden in our house. It seemed that the only words he knew had four letters. I hoped he and mama would never get back together again; he just took up more of her precious time,leaving less for me.

A month after I started school, the nurse suddenly appeared during reading time. She usually visited our class on Fridays, for the weekly bug check. On those days we were forced to line up and have our heads checked for lice with a wooden tongue depressor. I was so embarrassed when she searched my head for the detested bugs. I never failed to breathe an audible sigh of relief when my name was not included among those that were to be sent home with a note of instruction on how to get rid of the bugs. When a person was sent home with lice they weren't allowed to return to school until the nurse had checked their head and awarded them with a 'no-more bugs' slip. I felt sorry for those kids dismissed so abruptly although I laughed at them with everyone else. I knew one of these times I would take my place with them and be giggled and sneered at, because everyone seemed to take a turn in the bug line. I lived in dread of Friday afternoons it was the only day of the school week I disliked. Since this was Monday the nurse's appearance in our room was totally unexpected. She stood in the front of the class, her starched white uniform sticking out pointedly in all directions, telling us to line up. The nurse went on to explain that the doctor was on his way to administer our polio shots.

Everyone seemed to panic at once. My usually well behaved classmates and I flew into a frenzy. Miss Stevens and the pointed capped nurse tried to calm us down and round us up into some kind of order. Most of the kids were in tears, including me. I hated shots even more than I hated doctors. As I stood reluctantly in line behind my best friend, Margie, who was putting on a good show of bravery in spite of herself, I schemed about how to avoid the impending torture. When the doctor appeared, a moment later, looking larger than Superman, all havoc broke loose. The sounds of moans and wailing could be heard throughout the entire school. A few of the boys, who were putting on a show of toughness, were chosen to head the line and receive their abuse first. I stood there, head hung, eyes fixed on the black and grey linoleum, inching my way slowly towards the back of the line and waiting in dread for my turn.

The needle appeared to be at least eight inches long with a point as sharp as a shark's tooth as it loomed above the bony arms of my friends. As the ominous needle penetrated their frail arms the howling grew increasingly mournful and pained. When the nurse called my name, indicating it was my turn, my feet froze to the dulled tile. I couldn't move, I was petrified to the spot like an ancient rock that has been covered with layers of heavy soil. I felt Miss Stevens put her arm around my shoulder, attempting to cajole me into submission, still I could not move a muscle in my body. Quite suddenly I had more than enough energy, I ran around the class like a mad dog. I leapt over desks and under the teacher's chair. The nurse was hot on my trail as I bounded out the door and screamed all the way down the long hall. Just as I was almost out the main door and into the safety of the street, I felt a large pair of strong hands grabbing me and lifting me up high. I fought and yelled to no avail. I had been defeated in my race for freedom. I was going to be tortured like everyone else. The principal carried me back to class and held me securely as the doctor injected me with the vile serum.

After school it seemed that everyone had heard the tale of my great escape attempt. For days I was the main topic of conversation in the playground. For a while I was a hero of sorts.

My brothers and sister and I had a lot of responsibility. Debbie was placed in an adult role long before her time. She was the one responsible for running the house while mama was gone. She cooked and cleaned and cared for me as if she were my parent. It appeared that Debbie was extremely resentful and angry about this role she had to play with me and took every opportunity to punish me for it. Her favorite way of hurting me was to twist my arm so I would scream my head off and contort wildly to free myself. Sometimes she left dark purple bruises on the inside of my arms the exact shape of her hand. Once she even fed me dog food. Although she apologized and said she was only playing a joke when I told mama, it was an example of her anger at being mother to her younger sister.

Jimmy and David were vague and mysterious to me. Since they were not required to help out much at home, except to take the trash out once a week, they were hardly ever around except at dinner time. Jimmy had developed into a tall, attractive teenager. With his wavy black hair, dark penetrating eyes and olive skin he had quickly become the most popular guy with the girls in the neighborhood. When David and Jimmy were home they always were arguing about some girl they both liked. David was not as handsome as his older brother and he competed by using his sharp wit and intelligence rather than his average looks. Whenever I passed them on the street corner there seemed to be plenty of girls to go around. Though they fought a lot, Jimmy and David were always together and when one got in trouble for something the other was there with a good defense.

We also had quite a bit of freedom, as did most of the kids on our block. I belonged to a gang of about ten kids that roamed the streets and rode buses all over the city until it was dark and we had to go home for dinner. One of our favorite hangouts was the local settlement house a few blocks away. At any time of the day or night one of my brothers or sister was sure to be there along with most of my friends. We played games, made craft projects, got involved with sports or just hung around and bugged the counselors. I took piano and cooking lessons there as well as participating in other activities.

At Christmas time we would put on a pageant and invite our families for the show and cookies and tea. One year I was chosen to play Mary: I think it was the best performance ever. Debbie and I had some big battles at the settlement house. She would yell at me because she had to leave earlier than I did. It made her mad that she had to go home and cook supper before mama got home from work. I was just glad it wasn't me.

Grandpa John and Grandma Sarah lived only eight rowhouses down the street from us and were supposed to be in charge of me after school. I didn't spend much time there because it was usually more fun to be outdoors with my friends. My pals and I formed exclusive clubs whose membership changed daily according to who possessed the current popularity vote. We all played and fought energetically, wearing ourselves out just in time to go home for dinner and bed.

When I did spend time with my grandparents Grandma Sarah was usually downstairs in the kitchen cooking something that smelled delicious or visiting with someone from church. I spent most of my time with Grandpa John who didn't work regular hours and was often at home.

Grandpa John seemed to always want to hold me on his lap, especially when we were alone. He would lift me up into his wide lap and hold me tightly in his strong arms. I really enjoyed setting on grandpa's lap, feeling his warm loving while he told me silly stories of a magical chain inside his toothless mouth that lowered invisible teeth or of his horse that froze to death in a field of popping corn. Grandpa could always make me laugh. His tales didn't make much sense but they were very funny and I believed each and every one. Sometimes grandpa would tickle me all over while he held me. He seemed to enjoy my childish laughter as much as I delighted in his affectionate attention. Grandpa told me over and over how much he loved me. He would whisper softly in my ear, with a soothingly hypnotic voice, that I was his own special little girl, I would squirm and wiggle in his lap, trying to get even closer to this wonderful grandfather of mine. The specialness I felt with him and the loving and security of his arms around me made me feel warm all over. Maybe mama was too busy or too tired to give me the nurturance I craved but Grandpa John was always there wanting to hold me close.

My beloved grandfather, tall, blue-eyed, broad shouldered and strong, smelling of aftershave and soap. Bouncing when he walks, his voice loud and boisterous. My comical grandfather who always has a silly grin on his face and a humorous story or trick to make us laugh. He is never without a cheerful hello and a joke or two to share with everyone he meets. I believe Grandpa John is the funniest, kindest, most clever man in the world. In many ways he is the father I've never had. I always laugh until I cry at the foolish stories he tells over and over again. Just a glance at this marvelous man makes me light up with childish delight. It seems that everyone loves my grandfather, they always look so happy to see him pass by. He knows everyone in our neighborhood and although he doesn't have any real close friends everyone is his buddy or pal. I am the envy of my friends, to have such a fun-loving grandfather is a rare and special treat.

My gentle, sensitive grandfather whose favorite means of employment is to dress up in silly costumes and entertain us children. My sweet, wonderful grandfather, leader of the family and idol of his two daughters and five grandchildren. My darling, carefree grandfather, the admired and respected member of his church and community. Everyone loves my grandpa, especially me. He is my hero, my knight in shining armor. I am so proud that he belongs to me. My perfect grandfather, always here to hold me on his lap and give me the love I crave.

Grandpa John and I both have a passion for ice cream. When we walk through the neighborhood together to the local market for an ice cream cone I am the proudest little girl on earth. I feel just like a princess walking with my hand in his. I hold my head up high and show off my princely grandfather.

A special treat for me is when grandpa puts on his clown outfit and appears at the Saturday afternoon children's matinee around the corner from our house. He captivates us all with hilarious jokes and magic tricks. I, of course, am his biggest fan, laughing wildly at all of his silly antics. On the day he is to appear I make sure to be the first kid in line so I can get a front row seat. Sometimes he picks me out of the crowded theatre with a wink and a smile meant only for me and I glow with pride and joy. I feel so special because he loves me best of all. My friends just laugh and tell me they wished they had a grandfather just like mine.

Another of my favorite times is Christmas. Grandpa dresses up like Santa Claus and works as a helper at one of the big department stores uptown. My best friend, Margie, and I take the bus and go and see him as much as possible. Margie knows that he is really my grandpa and not Santa, that's what makes it so neat for me. I boast about him to everyone in line, which grandpa says I shouldn't do because it might make the store manager mad, but I do it anyway because I am so proud to be his grand-daughter. Sometimes, if he spends more time than usual with another child I get really jealous. Watching the other children sit on his lap and whisper in his ear is kind of difficult for me until I make myself remember that this is just his job and I am his only special little girl.

While playing outside with my friends I watch for his return home, waiting to see his funny face and jaunty step turn the cor-ner of our street. I run down the street to greet him, hoping he will pick me up and give me a big bear hug so the other kids will see how important I am, but he usually doesn't. He just gives us all a wide smile and a cheery hello. I need my friends to see how special I am to this wonderful man but he rarely gives me special attention when others are around. It's the same way at home. When other family members are present he pays no more atten-tion to me than the anyone else, in fact it seems that he gives me less. Most of the time grandpa appears to be either angry or sad when he is at home. He seems to talk around people rather than to them. He communicates through jokes or silence. Grandma Sarah nags him a lot, usually about his irresponsible work habits. I always side with grandpa, though silently, and feel angry at her for picking on him. In my eyes, grandpa can do no wrong.

When grandpa is in one of his bad moods he hardly acknow-ledges me with a look or a touch. I feel real panicky during these times. I always believe I have done something terribly wrong. I am totally convinced that it is all my fault that grandpa is so sul-len. Because if he loves me and if I am good enough he won't behave in such a grumpy way. I get so afraid he doesn't love me and that I am really not his special little girl. The rest of the family simply ignores him during his withdrawn times but for me these days are agony. Sometimes Grandpa John draws away for a few hours. Other times he is reclusive for several days. I am always there, waiting anxiously for my loving grandpa to come back and hold me tenderly. When he finally does return to his jovial old self again he acts as though nothing has happened and it's confusing to me. When we are alone he gives me a bear hug and reassures me that I am still his special one. As he holds me on his lap, enveloping me in his powerful arms, I know I am okay. I am safe. I am loved. I'm grandpa's special girl again.

I feel more comfortable, more at home, at my grandparents than I do in the house I share with my mom and brothers and sister. At my house there is hardly ever any one around. My mother seems to be gone all the time and just like my two brothers only comes home to eat and sleep. Debbie is gone as much as she can possibly manage and when she is home she is always trying to clean something up or cook dinner so as not to get mama mad at her. Just eight houses down the street is Grandma Sarah, usually baking something delicious, like my favorite gingerbread with whipped cream. Her kitchen always feels so warm and welcoming, but most of all I like to spend time there because Grandpa John is there to make me laugh and feel wanted.

My grandparents are usually in different parts of their three story rowhouse. She is usually downstairs in the kitchen cooking or visiting with friends while he watches TV or reads the newspaper in the living room upstairs. I love to crawl up into grandpa's lap and watch television or scoot under the paper and demand he pay attention to me. I have learned that I can only be this close to him when there is no one around, otherwise he will quickly shoo me off his lap. It is these quiet moments alone with grandpa that have come to mean so much to me. When I sit on his lap I don't feel lonely, or afraid. I belong, I feel important. It is almost as good as belonging to my mama who isn't really there for me.

It is during my sixth year, that my grandpa and I are spending more and more time alone together. He is babysitting much more frequently and our lap sitting time is increasing and beginning to take a different course. I love sitting on his lap, basking in the warmth of his soft touch. I am, by now, used to his gentle massaging of my arms, legs and torso. I have come to really enjoy this part of our times together, his hands feel so soothing that for just a moment I can actually feel secure.

I am sitting on grandpa's wide lap and watching Donald Duck cartoons. He is touching me beyond what is usual or expected. His large hand is reaching down, down further and further to stroke the inside of my thighs. His touch feels so ticklish that I am laughing. Slowly, stealthily he is slipping his hand under my short dress and cupping my genital area with his palm. He is rubbing his hand all over my private parts, as mother taught me to call them. He is whispering softly, almost inaudibly, in my ear, "I love you sweetheart, you're so special to me." His caress feels so strange, so different than anything I've ever known before, yet so tingly and warm. "Does that feel good Jenny? Do you like grandpa to touch you there?" My tongue refuses to answer; I am shaking my head slightly as he squeezes me tighter against his thighs and continues to touch me. We are sitting here, so wrapped up as one, my head resting securely against his chest as I stare through glazed eyes at the nonsensical television show. Grandma is calling his name from somewhere that feels far away. Grandpa John is kissing me on the cheek, patting my bottom and sending me out to play.

I never really thought much about what went on between me and grandpa although I often recalled the feeling and the heated wave-like sensations he aroused in my private parts. Sometimes while I lay wake in the darkness of my room I tried to recreate the ticklish warmth with my own hands but it never felt quite the same. I never stopped to think about whether what grandpa did with me was right or wrong as it was totally unbelievable to me that he could do anything that wasn't perfect.

At this time in my young life I knew next to nothing about the mysterious thing called sex, which was a forbidden topic in our conservative Baptist home. I don't think I even knew the word existed. The limited information I did possess came from the vague and hushed secrets my friends and I whispered about in the darkness of each other's rooms and clubhouses. My friends were much wiser that I in this area since they had parents to spy on. I did not have this educational opportunity since my mom and Peter had broken up. Even before that there had been very little for my curious eyes and ears. I did not connect the things my friends said with the loving and tenderness my grandfather showed.

Grandpa John was the daddy I never had. He was the only person I could count on to love me and not tell me to leave him alone all the time. Sometimes mama told me wonderful stories about my real daddy. My favorite was about him naming me and taking care of me when I was just a little baby. Mama always had tears in her eyes when she talked about my daddy, she tried to hide them with the palms of her hands but I saw them anyway. I felt so sad and kind of lost when she spoke of him but it was also one of the few times that mama took time to hold me and I sure liked that. Mama seemed to be sad so often when I was young. Sometimes I would watch her across the room and wonder why it was her brown eyes were so misted or why her prominent mouth was always slightly set in a frown. Maybe it was because she was such an unhappy kid herself, forever in competition with her younger sister, Lorraine, for her parent's too little money and attention. Or maybe her sad look was due to the loss of her husband when she was only twenty-six. I don't know whether any of this was real for mama, I only know that I always felt sorry for her, always felt as though I needed to take care of her. She appeared so fragile and needy, so powerless in a world that threatened to crumble at her feet. Somehow mama's sadness was forever beyond my help. No matter how hard I tried to make her happy she seemed troubled and lonely. I wanted to make the pain go away, to make her face shine with joy for just a moment but her brown eyes continued to be a mysterious well of pain and loneliness.

Once in awhile mama and I would sit together on the couch and she would tell me about how she met my daddy. I think that was her favorite story since she told it so much. When she spoke of falling in love with him at fifteen and marrying several months later her eyes shone like clear clean glass with sun pouring through. I liked to see mama's eyes like that, it made me think that maybe at one time she had been really happy. Mama talked about daddy's dreams of becoming rich and famous. She told me how gentle and kind he was and best of all, that he loved me best of all his children. She said daddy was totally excited about my being born and spent the last two years of his life caring for me while she worked to support the family. Sometimes she told me sad stories about daddy being sick and in and out of the hospital over the last five years of his life. I didn't like to hear all that and I pretended that daddy was away making movies in foreign countries and would return home any day. I hated hearing her say my daddy was dead.

She told me that even though I had known daddy the least amount of time that I seemed to love him more than the other kids. Mama told me that when he died and grandma and grandpa drove to Chicago to take us home to New York that I screamed non stop the entire four day drive. She said that nothing she tried would pacify me and that I yelled for "da-da" all the way.

Mama liked to tell stories about grandpa too. Her favorite one was about how grandpa taught her to develop film and do all the things she does in the darkroom at work. It was obvious that mama loved grandpa as much as I did, though she often said that he needed to grow up and not be such a burden to grandma. I wasn't sure what she meant by that but I believed that it was the only negative comment she ever made about him. Mama told me to be nice to grandpa and help grandma out around the house whenever I could. She said they were the best parents in the world but I told her that I thought she was. She smiled and said she wished she were. I asked mama to play with me but she was too tired or had another errand to run. Mama was always very busy or tired. Once I asked her where babies came from and she turned all red in the face and told me that a big white stork delivered them to special people who really wanted them. She said she wanted me even though she hadn't been planning on having another baby and was very surprised when she found out I was coming. That story never made much sense to me but mama was mama and I knew she had all the answers.

During my second year of school Grandma Sarah became very ill. I decided to spend as much time with her as possible so I could help her around the house. I especially enjoyed helping her in the kitchen when she would bake my favorite dessert of gingerbread with whipped cream.

Grandma Sarah was a tall, stately woman with prematurely graying hair and deep set brown eyes. The wrinkles at the corners of her eyes made her look as though she was always on the verge of laughter, although I seldom saw her actually laugh. She seemed like a very serious person, somewhat distant and remote. Although she was not a warm, cuddly type of grandma, her soft way of speaking and gentle manner made her always pleasant to be around. Grandma, was the one I ran crying to when I needed bandaging. Mama would panic about my proneness to accidents but grandma was there with tender hands and comforting words.

Grandma was well liked and an esteemed member in our church and neighborhood. People seemed to seek her out for guidance and support. Nearly every afternoon there was someone sitting her kitchen asking for her help. I really liked it that people looked up to her. When I grew up I wanted people to need me like they did her. I know now that she was the unspoken leader of our matriarchal family. She covered up her husband's irresponsibility and inability to deal with adult tasks.

My grandmother gave me much attention for being both pretty and smart. She would tease me by saying that my cat-like green eyes and long brown hair made me pretty enough to be a model, except that I was too skinny. She often bragged to her afternoon guests about how well I did in school. Sometimes she used me as the subject when she was experimenting with new photographic equipment. Smiling into the camera for her was one of my favorite things to do; it made me feel as if I were important to her. Grandma Sarah was a quiet and unassuming woman who took great comfort in the teachings of the church. Her religious beliefs were her major source of strength and nourishment. Our whole family depended on her to be there for them. Whether it was to take one of her grandchildren to the doctor or loan money to her daughters, Grandma Sarah was the only one who was always there to take care of things. She was the backbone of the family. She was our stability and when she became ill with cancer our family became shaky and ungrounded.

Even with all my grandma's apparent strength she often seemed frail to me. Now that she was sick I was more guarded than usual with her. She spent most of her time lying down because walking had become difficult and painful. Many afternoons I played nurse for her, bringing her coffee and cookies and answering the telephone so she wouldn't have to get up herself. I now shielded grandma from my childhood troubles and injuries, going home to put on band-aids alone instead of running to her. Seeing her grow increasingly pale and disabled caused me to worry a lot. I was very afraid she might die, not so much for what it might mean to me as for the strength she gave to mama. I was sure that if grandma died so would my mother. Mama was especially needy and dependent on grandma and her long Illness was draining and stressful for her. Without constant assurance of her mother's love, mama was even more lonely and unsure of herself. She looked so sad and lost during grandma's long period of recovery and spent all her free time visiting her, either at the hospital or at home. I saw even less of mama than before.

Soon after Thanksgiving grandma was hospitalized for many months. Mama didn't want me to visit her because she said little kids shouldn't have to do such adult things, but I eventually convinced her to take me there. The first time I went to visit her was so frightening. Seeing her lying there helplessly with the intravenous tubes coming out of her body made me cry and run out of the room. I needed to believe she was still the pillar of strength and the fearless leader of our family. I realized then and there that she needed to be protected and taken care of. I left there feeling like something really bad was going to happen to our family if grandma didn't hurry up and get better.

The more time mama spent with grandma the more jealous and resentful I became. I felt like all she cared about was Grandma Sarah. I had been begging her for more time and now I wasn't even getting as much as before. She no longer seemed interested in how well I did in school or how cute I could be. She didn't seem to know I existed. I grew more lonely and needy with each passing day. As mama's time and energy at home lessened, Debbie's responsibilities increased to the point that she was in full charge of running the house. Her anger seemed to fill the house like a hot dry wind that threatened to break down the walls. Since I was the only one smaller than her and so readily available, I quickly became the target of her burning rage. Debbie had long been overweight but now she grew heavier and got more hostile everyday. When mom was home she and Debbie did "head on battle" which usually resulted in my sister stomping out of the room and slamming the door loudly behind her. Mama obviously didn't know what to do with her, since she did nothing. Jimmy and David were rarely at home and I had little contact with them except in passing on the street or at the settlement house once in a while.

I became more and more demanding and whiny. When mama was home I followed her around the house begging her for attention. I became mom's shadow, chasing her from room to room, complaining all the way. She was too self-absorbed to see my mounting needs as anything more than a nuisance. She responded to my pleas for her time and love by sending me outside to play or to my room to think about why I was being so bad. I tried finding ways to make myself less lonely but what I actually did was become withdrawn. I played with my friends less often, choosing to visit Grandpa John or stay home and read instead. Many afternoons I spent out on the upstairs fire escape; I would arrange pillows and blankets comfortably in order to indulge my favorite solitary pastime. Many days I sat there until sunset savoring each passage of a treasured novel. My Great-grandmother, Mary Elizabeth, had taught me to read when I was three and I had been addicted to discovering new worlds through books ever since. My fascination with stories gave me a means to escape some of the loneliness and despair I was experiencing more and more often.

Tossing fitfully, rolling over to embrace the wall I think to myself, "No it's too early, don't want to wake up yet, just let me sleep, mama, please."

The light from the hallway is too bright, it is hurting my eyes. Tickling fingers on my leg send chilled shivers up my spine. Pushing the hair back from my dream clouded eyes to find Grandpa John sitting here on the edge of my bed. The room is darkened, the only light is from the hallway, casting ghostly shadows across his face. I can see that his body is close, and that he is staring with eyes that appear to be misty and empty with loneliness. His body is close to mine, I feel the heat of it reaching out to me, it is somehow both stifling and welcome. His largeness looms over me as his shadow envelops the small bed where I lie in waiting. I am happy to see him yet the fear that has begun to grow is there lodged in my chest like an apple core swallowed by mistake.

"What time is it grandpa? What are you doing here?" My voice arises from the depths of sleepiness to surprise us both.

He smiles slowly, the type that always seems to come from some unexpected pleasure. His words are whispered so low that I must move closer to hear them. "I came to see my favorite little person, honey. Don't worry about the time, it's okay. I just missed you and wanted to talk a little, okay baby?"

"Sure grandpa but where's mama? Did she send you up here to check on me or something?" I am confused, I don't know why he is here or what he wants. And where is mama?

"Don't worry about your mother, she's just fine. She's down at my house with grandma. She won't be back for awhile yet." His voice has taken on that soft ooziness that has now become all too familiar to me. "You look so cute and sweet all dressed in your little pajamas. Do you know that you are the prettiest little girl that ever lived? Do you know how much grandpa loves you? I do, you know more than anyone else ever has or ever will." His gentle words are tenderly wrapping themselves around me. His loving surrounds me with safety. "Do you know how special you are to me Jenny? Do you know how much I love you?" His words are pleading with me to love him too.

"I think so grandpa. I love you too, you know." My own words are whispered breathlessly as he is pulling me up into his lap.

"Oh Jen, you are such a beautiful little woman, I just love to hold you and touch your soft skin. Can I rub you a little bit honey? It would make me feel so good, okay baby?" There is no need for me to answer as his rough hands have already begun traveling over my arms, down my chest and over the flatness of my belly. On and on down towards the tickle spot between my legs. His touch feels as delicate as butterfly wings against my cheek. As he caresses me he slowly murmurs quietly into my ear. "My coming to see you tonight is our special secret honey, okay? Just like when we sit together. It's important that you never forget that Jenny. I don't want you to tell your mama or anyone else, okay Jen? This is our own special time, just for us, right baby?"

"Sure grandpa, but why?" My head is spinning now, his long fingers probing my tickle place. I don't understand why he doesn't want me to tell anyone. Is there something wrong with his being here? Would mama get mad at me again if she found out?

"It's nothing for you to worry your pretty little head about honey. Just relax and promise me that we can keep this as part of our own special secret. I'll take good care of you honey, don't I always? I even have a brand new dollar bill for you in my pocket, okay Jen?" His voice is now muffled and strained against my hair. "Now you must promise Jen. You be the good little girl that I know you want to be okay?" I nod my head on his shoulder as his grip on me tightens. He is stroking my thighs oh so softly that it is as if a feather were being trailed in tiny circles. He is sighing quietly, the warmth of his love covering me delicately as I drift back to sleep with grandpa's hands between my legs.

When I awoke the next morning he was gone. I lay in bed look-ing at the spot where I had thought he had been, trying to figure out whether he had really been there or if perhaps I had dreamed the whole thing. My eyes caught sight of a crisp one dollar bill resting on the corner of my dresser. As it turned out this night-time visit was only the first of many to come.

I hated it when grandpa was in one of his down moods. I wanted so badly to make him happy. I tried to please him so that he would laugh and joke with me in his special way. I never imagined there was anything unusual about the way he loved me. I just figured it must be alright since no one had ever told me differently. It felt so good that it couldn't possibly be wrong. I didn't question why he kept calling our times together our own secret or why he made me promise not to tell anyone. So I kept my word and never mentioned it to anyone.

I needed to feel loved by someone and I believed that grandpa loved me. All that was important was that he continued to hold and love me. When we were alone, while caressing my body, he would speak of the love he felt for me in his strange sounding voice. He always asked for assurance that I loved him too. Some-times he would ask me repeatedly to tell him of my love, saying he liked hearing it over and over again.

While sitting on his lap being fondled, I gradually become aware of something hard underneath me but I never asked what it was. I think I was a little afraid of the strange hardness under my bottom. Once in awhile he would reach under me and touch it for a minute or two. One day while we were sitting together he asked me to touch him too. Up until now I always sat passively while he stroked me. I eagerly responded and rubbed his back until my arms ached. I asked him repeatedly if it felt good, just as he always did with me. When he moaned a soft yes in reply it made me feel real good. A few moments later my mother came into the room and told me what, a good girl I was to rub grand-pa's back for him.

At home I was doing everything I possibly could to get mother to pay more attention to me. I soon learned that if I cried long enough she would break down and hold me for a brief moment before rushing off to her next task. I felt so cut off from her I was as though there was a barrier between us that I could never quite get through. My manipulative nature developed very quickly and I became an even more demanding child, always wanting more affection. I felt as though I could never get enough nurturance. I worshipped my mother, or rather, the idea of a mother. It seemed as if I was always trying to get her to fit my mold of the perfect mom, like the ones on TV. I was full of fears, always checking under the bed for the bogeyman and kidnappers. My worst fear was that my mom wouldn't come home from work at all and that I would be stuck with my sister as a full time parent.

It was during my grandmother's long illness that Grandpa's advances became increasingly more sexual. He was not available to me as much as in the past but whenever we were able to be together he seemed eager to be near me. Without my grandma or mother around to meet any of my needs I reached out to grandpa even more.

His night visits to my room continued over the following months as did our lap-sitting ritual. It was now fairly routine that when I sat on grandpa's lap or next to him on the couch that he would fondle my body, including my genitals. I hungered for his reassuring love and attention. I assumed all grandfathers loved their granddaughters this way, although usually I didn't think about it at all.

Grandma is home from the hospital, she is lying on the couch downstairs. Grandpa and I are watching TV he is holding me on his lap and caressing me softly. He is whispering, "Oh Jenny, I love you so much." I am caught somewhere between the glow of the television and the comfort of his massaging hands. My eyes are glazed and clouded as I squirm to get even closer to the words that roll over and over before encasing me in their tenderness. "You're so wonderful my little darling, don't ever go away from me. I couldn't live without you Jenny."

I reply in the same tone as his, one that seems to hypnotize us to this moment, "I love you too grandpa. I'll never leave you, don't worry." He is rubbing my thighs and genitals, sending tingles through my body.

He is asking me questions that make me feel embarrassed somehow, "Does that feel good honey, or do you want me to do it harder or slower?" I can't reply, I hate these questions. I like it best when he doesn't talk at all. "Tell me what it feels like honey, I want to know what you like best." His words are demanding, interrupting the spell he has cast. I am alone now, trying in vain to say whatever it is he wants to hear. Now all I want is to watch the cartoons that are dancing before me. "Come on Jenny tell grandpa what you like, please honey, it would make me so happy."

I stutter, trip and stumble over the words I do not know. "I don't know grandpa, it just kinda tickles and stuff." I am rescued by the sound of grandma calling from downstairs.

He is muttering while pushing me off and adjusting his pants, "Wait right here, I'll be right back." I sit alone in his big chair engulfed by its emptiness. I am trying not to wait but I'm waiting none the less. The distance between me and the television feels as vast as the train station downtown. I am left with glassy eyes that can't focus on Mickey Mouse and his friends. I hear the heaviness of grandpa's return coming up the steps, my body quickens as though an earthquake is showing its first power. "Come here Jen."

He is standing by the door, he looks like a giant, I don't know how, but he has grown at least two feet since he left. I walk slowly to him, he is wrapping me in his arms, lifting me up and inching at a snail's pace back to the chair. We are here again, sitting in the place we are supposed to be, entwined needs with nowhere else to go. "Touch me here Jen, please baby." He is pulling my hand down to the crotch of his pants, holding it as if it must be there. I am scared, I feel my throat close over my protests. I have never been asked to do this before, what does it mean, what does he want? I want to please him, I need to. I am letting him guide my tiny hand with his own over his bulging pants. I am feeling for the first time, the hard object that has been under my bottom so many times before. It feels strange, hard yet very soft too. He is unzipping his pants and placing my hand directly on his on his stained underwear. "Oh Jen that feels so good." His moans are soft and wet, leaving traces of spittle on my ear. I don't like the way his voice is making me feel. He is doing something with his hand, pulling something out from his underwear. Oh God, it is long and ugly, it looks like a big white worm. I am startled and quickly pull my hand away. "It's okay Jenny," he assures me in his most oozing voice. "It's just my penis, It won't hurt you I promise. I'd really like you to touch it a little, it'll make me feel so good, okay honey?"

"I'm scared grandpa," I am trying to make my words sound big but they are coming from too far down to sound anything but muffled. I can feel myself shrinking, getting smaller and smaller as each moment passes.

"It's alright Jen, really. I love you and I Just want you to love me like I do you. Here, just touch it a minute, okay?" I am so frightened, I don't think I am supposed to do this but he is my grandpa so it must be alright. I hesitate and bury my head in his shoulder.

"Come on honey, it's really okay, Here, let me have your hand and I'll show you how to love me." It feels as though he is begging me. He holds my hand in his and teaches me how to caress his penis in the way that gives him pleasure. "Ahh yes, that's right, yes. That's real good, a little faster now honey, yeah that's great." I am watching him, immobilized, except for my hand that he is guiding over his body. I am afraid, yet, I am also fascinated by the changes that are taking place in him. He is breathing very loudly, his breath is hot and heavy on my neck. His body is tense and his face is turning different shades of red.

"What's wrong grandpa?" I am afraid he is sick or something, he certainly looks ill or upset, in fact he is the same color he gets when grandma is yelling at him.

"Nothing, nothing," he pants heavily,"I'm fine. It feels real good, don't stop." His penis seems to ge growing bigger and harder in my hand. It feels real squishy and weird, I don't like touching it but grandpa says he wants me to, so I guess I better do it. His chest is rising and he is clutching the arm of the chair.

"Are you okay grandpa? Do you want me to stop now?"

"No don't stop. It feels so good. It feels like how you feel when, I touch you down there, know what I mean honey?" I know what he's talking about, it is that strange ticklish. sensation that always makes me squirm in his lap. I am kind of happy to make grandpa feel that funny feeling. He is lying with his head. resting on the back of the chair, a small smile has spread over his face, he is moaning softly, my arm is so tired but he is telling me not to stop over and over again. Suddenly he is jumping up and pulling himself away from me.

"Go outside and play now!", he says loudly while he zips up his pants. "I'll see you later." I am sure I have done something terribly wrong, he looks angry with me. I am feeling so alone and afraid as he heads up the stairs to the bathroom, I am sitting here again, trapped in the big chair that was never meant for one little person. My head is spinning with dark colors and through the ringing I hear Grandma Sarah calling from downstairs. I force my legs to unwind from beneath my dress and brace my arms to lift my weight from the chair. Carefully, I find my balance and make my way to the voice below.

"What in the hell are you doing here? I told you to go outside. Now go on, get out of here right now!" His once calm, loving tones are gone and replaced by a harshness usually reserved for grandma.

"Are you mad at me grandpa?" My own voice is distant and meek.

"No girl, but you better do what I tell you to and right now! Get out of here and on the double!"

I am running as fast as I can. Down the street filled with old ladies carrying shopping bags and small children with smudgy faces. I burst through my door and run up the stairs two at a time. I am so scared, so confused that I can't seem to get the window unlocked. Finally it gives and lets me climb out to the safety of my fire escape home. I am still. Staring at the sky until I blend with the clouds and all that is real up there. I don't understand what has just happened with grandpa and me. I am so scared, why is he mad at me?, Why did he yell at me and tell me to leave like that? I know he doesn't love me anymore, I am a bad little girl. It feels like something important has changed but I can't figure out what it is. I wish I could fly like the birds high above me, I would fly away and rest on the cloud's softness. Tears are coming, I feel them fighting to be free, they are rolling down my cheeks and landing in pools on my scabbed knees. My sister came home to find me still sitting on the fire escape long after the sun had set.

May 29, 1960

Dear Diary,

Today I am eight years old. Grandpa John gave me this diary for my birthday. Mama had a party and we played games and

*had a big cake and lots of chocolate ice cream. It was really fun.
I wanted a bicycle but mama says she's afraid I'll get run over
so she gave me a doll and two books instead. I like this diary
best of all. I'm gonna write in it everyday and then hide it
under my bed so Debbie won't read it.*

June 12, 1960

Dear Diary,

*Debbie and I are going to camp tomorrow with the Petersons
from church. I'm kind of scared to go but mama says I can
learn to ride a bike up there so I guess I'll go. Debbie is being
really mean lately and she said that when we're at camp she's
not even gonna talk to me. I don't know why she always gets
mad at me when mama gets mad at her but she sure does. Peter
came over to see mama last night. I sure hope he doesn't come
back to live with us because I hate him, he always makes mama
cry.*

———————————

Camp turned out to be a cottage located in a beautiful wooded
area just a few yards from a large lake. Aunt Susan, as we were
told to call Mrs. Peterson, was kind and devoted much of her
time and energy to the children she was fostering for the summer. Mr. Peterson was usually outside busily working around
the house or yard and I had very little contact with him. Sometimes he looked at me, his eyes catching mine across the dinner
table, lingering a disturbing second too long. I felt awkward and
embarrassed. I would feel a flush of heat redden my face, I didn't
know why, I just did. Soon I became friends with Sally and Connie, the two girls I shared a room with. We spent our days roam-
ing through the forest, learning to ride two-wheelers, swimming,
picnicking and playing along the lake shore. Together we played

from early morning until sundown, falling into our beds sun-burnt and exhausted.

I felt carefree and happy in this peaceful setting. Mama was gone so much of the time before I had left that I was fairly used to being without her so I hardly missed her at all. Sometimes I wished grandpa would come and see me, but just for a moment or two. I wanted to show off my funny grandpa to my new friends but I was scared of him showing me too much attention also. Lately it seemed that he wanted me to spend all my time with him and I was having too much fun now to want to do that.

Connie and Sally were both two years older than I and they seemed to know much more about the ways of the world than I did. Through them I learned some invaluable, and very fright-ening information about sex. Tucked into our cots, we whispered and giggled into the late evening hours, eventually making our way to the fascinating subject of sex. Though they seemed to be more informed, I soon discovered that I really knew more about it than they did. I worked hard at never letting them know this, always pretending to be more naive than I actually was.

They described people touching each other's private places and long intense kisses in great detail. Connie had even seen her parents "doing it", as I then learned to call it. She explained how her father was lying on top of her mother and going up and down. She laughed uproariously when she told of their moans and grunting sounds. Both girls told their stories repeatedly, laughing all the while. In the beginning I was repulsed but curi-ous and asked for more and more information. The more they described their parent's behavior the more confused I became. A knot in the pit of my stomach churned painfully. I felt dizzy and out of focus, my head swirled as if I were riding the tilt-a-whirl at Coney Island. Flashes of images confronted and haunted me; grandpa with his mouth buried between my legs the strain of his heavy breathing, the mournful sound of his groans against my neck. Connie told of seeing her dad's penis while visions of grandpa, touching his, blinded me.

Not understanding what was happening to me, I felt panicked and alone. Why did the sexual behavior they described sound so familiar to me? I was just a little girl, I wasn't supposed to know anything about that stuff, they even said so. Why did I feel nervous and start stuttering when they talked of kissing and touching? What was wrong with me? I felt as though I were spiraling down, down into a deep dark hole that threatened to suffocate me. I didn't know what to think, I didn't know how I felt, I thought maybe I was going crazy. I knew grandpa loved me in a special way, he told me that often enough, but I didn't know until now that his loving me was called sex and that sex was ugly and dirty. Was it wrong then, were the caresses that felt so good really wrong? Why would grandpa do something that everyone thought was terrible? I thought he loved me, I needed him to love me, no one else did.

Now while they chatted on and on, repeating the same horror filled stories, I pretended to be asleep. Cowering under my blankets, my head hidden by the pillow, hands covering my ears, trying desperately not to hear, not to see the images of grandpa's loving. Their words droned on, reverberating through the layers of protection I tried to build for myself. At last when they had given up for the night, I lay alone, clutching my knees to my chest, rocking slowly until sleep took me to the land of my nightmares. Grandpa is here, sitting by my side, his large hands rubbing me rhythmically. His words soothing and lovingly tender. His face soft and smiling as he undoes his pants and moves my small hand to cover his need. I am touching him, feeling joy in my role as giver of pleasure to my wonderful grandfather. I hear laughter, jeering, curses of anger and humiliation coming from the doorway. Sally and Connie are here, their fingers pointing, their mouths turned up in ridicule.

I wake up to the sounds of my own screams, Aunt Susan, is here by my side, probing, "What's wrong Jenny, what in the world could possibly scare you so?"

"Nothing." How could I possibly tell her that what I am learning must never be told. She leaves me alone to wait for more images of the grandfather whose love is becoming my personal torture.

The summer moved so slowly. I could no longer let myself be with my friends, every minute I was forced to spend with them meant a possible chance for them to discover my nasty secret. I stayed to myself as much as Aunt Susan would allow. I often wandered into the countryside to think and hide from the ugliness I was discovering about myself and my life. Sitting under the protective shade of a large elm I wondered obsessively about grandpa's loving. Why did he do things to me that only married people were supposed to do? Why did it feel so good if it was so wrong?

I must be the worst person in the world. It was all my fault, I had let him touch me in ways that he wasn't supposed to. God would surely punish me and send me to hell. I wanted and needed to hide from myself and everyone else, but no matter what I did I could not free myself from the prison of my memories. I didn't understand. Grandpa John loved me, didn't he? Didn't other grandfathers love their granddaughters like mine did me? Why did my friends say his loving was naughty? I grew increasingly listless and unresponsive. Nothing was any fun. Food was repulsive, people too threatening and scary.

The shame I experienced daily drove me further inward. I was alone and lonely. I wouldn't let anyone near me. I was terrified they would find out about my bad sins. I barely spoke, I was so afraid I might slip and give my secret away. I kept my eyes cast downward and my shoulders grew curved and slouched. Thoughts of God's wrath tormented me. I pictured myself burning in hell eternally. Aunt Susan tried to reach out to me, she kept after me, trying to find out why I had suddenly become so quiet and sullen. I yearned to curl up in her arms and pour out my secrets, but I knew I couldn't. I was trapped by my own fear and guilt. I fended her off with feeble excuses that she seemed to believe.

My sister, Debbie, avoided me during that long summer of change. She was finally free of her parental responsibilities and she took full advantage of it. When I did try to be near her she became angry and aloof, telling me to quit bugging her. She didn't seem to notice or care about the dramatic changes that were taking place in me. I remained alone throughout the remaining weeks of summer camp. The other kids seemed fed up with my isolation and no longer sought me out to play. Most days I sat under a tree by the lake, reading books or simply staring at the water as the wind rippled over its surface. At night I lay awake, obsessed with the ugliness of my world until the blackness of sleep exploded into more dreams of my past days with grandpa.

As if sitting on a cloud floating high above the lake, I watched my summer sentence pass as if in slow motion. Yet all too soon the air began to chill slightly and suitcases were packed for the trip home. I didn't want to see my mother but most of all, I was terror stricken at the thought of seeing grandpa again. As the day approached for mother to pick me up I lay on my cloud fantasizing ways in which I could run away and never return to Columbus Avenue and Grandpa John.

The dreaded day arrived, too soon, the sun peaking its way through the window as if to alert me that it was time to go. I dressed quietly while the rest of the cottage slept, oblivious to my terror. With suitcase in hand, I ran to the trees that had shielded me from intimacy and schemed of ways to avoid going home. I had nowhere to go, no one to turn to. I felt totally helpless in a world that made no sense. I sat there, head buried in my lap, tears soaking my clothes, the taste of bile's bitterness strong in my mouth. Listening to mother and Debbie call my name in the distance I tried to become one with the tree, begging God to let me disappear into its trunk to safety. I was stuck, I couldn't run, my legs were stiff and immobile, I couldn't go towards them, my panic too strong. When I was discovered, covered with leaves and bark, eyes swollen shut, and my jaw clenched so tight it refused to budge, mother held me briefly saying how sad I must feel to leave such a wonderful summer paradise.

I hugged my mother, robot-like, and followed her haltingly to the car. She could not guess and was unable to understand the shattering fears that engulfed me. How could I tell her or anyone what I had learned on my summer vacation? How could I possibly share the secret that was slowly destroying me.

September 3, 1960

Dear Diary,

I've been home for three days, everything seems different somehow. Grandma is still sick and she is supposed to go back to the hospital soon. Mama has been working real late and only coming home for dinner before she goes down to grandma's house. She keeps after me to go with her but I don't want to. Debbie is being real mean to me again and David and Jimmy are never home.

September 10, 1960

Dear Diary,

Today I sat on the fire escape over the alley and read Little Women again. It is the most wonderful book, I wish I had a mother like they did. Margie came over to play but I didn't want to. Tomorrow I'm going to read the Five Little Peppers. Mama asked me if I were sick or something and I told her my stomach hurt a little. She said if I don't act better soon she will take me to the doctor so I better get better soon.

September 15, 1960

Dear Diary,

School started today. The third grade is so boring. My teacher, Mrs. Johnson is real weird. All my old friends say they are glad to see me, I didn't really care much about them. Oh well. Mrs. Johnson made us stand up and tell about our summer vacations, I don't know why but I started to cry so she sent me to the nurse. The nurse just sent me back to class but by that time they were done.

Being back at home was even worse than I had imagined it would be. It seemed as though everything had changed; maybe I just saw it differently. I was suspicious of everyone and everything. All I wanted was to be alone, to hide. I knew I had to keep away from people or they would discover the truth about me.

I avoided my grandfather whenever I could. At family gatherings I made sure to stay out of his reach. I never went into a room alone with him. I didn't look or talk with him. When he visited our house I quickly went upstairs to my room. The worst was when he babysat for me and my brothers and sister were out. If he tried to get me to talk to him or sit on his lap I locked myself in the bathroom until someone returned home. It seemed as though I wasn't safe anywhere, especially in my own house. I was painfully lonely. Mother was always too busy to pay much attention to me. Grandma Sarah was still ill and unable to attend my needs. No one seemed to notice the exile I had sentenced myself to. The attention I received for being whiny and tearful usually resulted in being sent to my room. I spent more and more time alone with my books. There was no one I wanted to pretend the summer has never happened and go back to being grandpa's special little girl. Even though I now knew his way of loving me was wrong, I still craved his attention.

Sometimes I even tried to act as though nothing had changed. So many times I wanted to snuggle up in grandpa's arms. I loved him yet I also hated him. I needed him and knew he was there but I couldn't go to him. Every time I was about to give into my longing for his tenderness I would remember Sally and Connie saying how nasty our loving was. As much as I wanted him to hold me and make me feel safe, I wouldn't go near him. The conflict was making my head spin.

When school started. and I entered third grade things were a little better. I tried to get involved with my studies. I tried to play with friends. I tried to forget my grandfather. Still, most of the time I felt as though there was a great weight around my neck causing me to sink into a gaping hole in the ground. I no longer cared about how I looked, forgetting to brush my hair and change my clothes regularly. I cringed when someone said I was pretty. I began taking frequent baths. At first it was only once a day, then it became two, three, and four times daily. I would lock the door and stay submerged beneath the water until someone banged on the door and insisted I come out. Unfortunately our house had only one bathroom otherwise I would probably have stayed there all the time. My once voracious appetite continued to decrease. If anyone noticed the changes in my behavior or appearance they never mentioned it to me. I felt sadder and more alone with each passing day.

More and more books were my respite. Reading was a pleasant and easy escape for me. For a short while I could leave my own cluttered world and become someone else, someone magical and free. My obsession with reading often got me in trouble. I started to wet the bed almost every night. The rule in our home was that when you wet the bed you were sent to bed at five o'clock with a peanut butter sandwich and were not seen or heard from until the next morning. Usually I welcomed this escape unto the relative safety of my bedroom and books. I would read by the window until I could no longer see and then use a flashlight under the blankets. When my mother would discover me doing this she would scold me profusely and take my books away. At these moments I hated her intensely. Leaving me alone with just my thoughts was my worst punishment.

During this time period I developed an active fantasy life. While lying in bed, with nothing else to do, I would imagine I lived in another world with a totally different family. This imaginary family resembled a combination of Beaver Cleaver's and the way of life on "Father Knows Best", with a little bit of "I Love Lucy" thrown in. My fantasy refuge quickly developed into a pattern and I began making ritualistic visits each evening. I'd imagine I was at school and the principal called me into his office. I was informed that everyone in my family had been killed in an accident. I had the logistics worked out to the smallest detail. Everyone, even distant relatives, had taken a bus trip. A bus was essential so that they would all fit in one place together and therefore be able to die together. On this trip their bus collided with a garbage truck and they had all perished immediately. I had them die quickly so I wouldn't feel too guilty about their suffering. The principal went on to tell me that I was being adopted by a kind couple that lived in the country. These fantasy people had no children and had always wanted a quiet, skinny girl just like me. The principal would then drive me to their mansion in the hills far away. It had a swimming pool and a horse.

I was greeted with hugs and kisses by the glowing couple who looked very much like Ward and June Cleaver, and from then on all my wishes came true. I was loved and wanted. Neither of my parents worked and they devoted all their time to me. I had no brothers or sisters to compete with for attention. I had no mother who was too busy for me. I didn't have a grandfather who did bad things to me. I was safe and happy.

From there my fantasy world would develop to include all the fun things I had ever wanted to do. Some nights I imagined we took trips to places like Disneyland or the mountains. Other times we stayed home and shared peaceful family dinners and then played games. Every aspect of this secure world was perfectly designed by me. I was happy with and depended on my imaginary world. My imagination provided me with a haven from confusion and fear.

Slowly waking, eyes blinking, stretching, feeling a weight on my leg. Fear is reality. Grandpa John is here, sitting on the edge of the bed, his hand on my thigh, his blue eyes piercing the darkness. Hiding, inching my way under the covers, I am trying to blend into the wall. I am holding my breath, my chest is distended and rock-like. My stomach is forcing its way up my constricted throat.

"I know you're not asleep Jen. I want to talk to you. Don't be afraid, tell me what's wrong with you. I've been so worried since you came home. I missed you so much when you were gone. How come you don't come to see me anymore?"

Grandpa's voice is all too familiar. I feel a grinding, pulsating sensation in my intestines. My saliva tastes salty, I can't swallow, can hardly breath. I crouch further and further under the blankets, tears are burning my eyes. Hugging my knees I rock rhythmically. Please take me away, oh wall, please open up and let me in. I can't tell him what I've learned. I love him, I hate him. I want him to go away, I need him to stay.

I am trying not to hear him as he croons so softly, "It's okay Jenny. Nothing's going to hurt you baby, grandpa is here to take care of you. Oh honey, I love you so much. You're grandpa's special little girl." He Is reaching out, his roughened hand straining to touch me. "Come up from under there and let me hold you, I've missed you so much. I need you Jenny, please. Come on now, come here and be with grandpa." His voice sounds edgy now as if he is on the brink of something he doesn't want to feel.

"NO! Go away! I hate you!" Tears flowing from my eyes, my chest heaving perilously. "Go away, please God make him go away," I pray.

I am clenching my pillow between my legs, I am trying to make the wall take me in. Where is God when I need him? His hands are on me, their weight a burden I can not carry. I am struggling, pushing my legs into his stomach, flailing my arms and fists. He is so strong, he has me, I am smothering in his body. I am helpless to his needs and my own. I can't take it, I need you too but you hurt me, you make me do things that are wrong, I don't want to go to Hell. My arms are wrapped tightly around my chest, I'm making sure my nightgown is pulled around my knees. He is rocking me gently while stroking my hair. His voice is coming through in distortions as if first going through a long tunnel. He is telling me my favorite stories. The one about when he was in the National Guard and stole pies off a window sill, yet his words don't make me laugh like before. I am beginning to feel safe, I don't want to. I wiggle and squirm. there is no release from the web of his arms, I am trapped in his love, I am engulfed by his desires. Time seems to have stopped, I am trying to count my heartbeats as they pound loudly in my temples. He talks and his words trip and tumble over me.

"Please baby, please tell me what is wrong with you. Don't you love me anymore? Aren't you still grandpa's little girl?"

His voice is smooth and deceptive, I want to trust him. I don't seem to have any other choice, yet I'm so scared to love him. Who is he? His whispers sound so real, so caring, so much like the grandpa I thought was gone forever. I am gasping, as my air is being funneled to my lungs so sluggishly. My words are pouring out in torrents of uncontrolled anguish. I am telling him all about Sally and Connie, all the details of my nightmarish summer. So many words blurted out in a moment of childish faith. He is listening, I can tell. He is rocking me gently, all the while.

"Honey there's nothing wrong with the way we love each other. Oh my poor baby, you've been all upset over nothing. You don't have to be married to love someone the way I do you. I'm just trying to teach you about loving now so that when you grow up you'll know what to do. Jenny you're the most important person in the world to me, I'd never do anything to hurt you. You know that don't you?"

"I don't know grandpa. I guess so, but why did they say it was bad then? I'm scared grandpa."

"Some people don't understand about this stuff like we do. They're just dumb kids anyway, who cares what they think. We have our own special secret, just between us. You mustn't tell anyone about our times together. They wouldn't understand and it would just make them jealous anyway. Do you understand? You know I love you and I'll always take good care of you, you'll just have to trust me Jenny. Don't worry about them or anyone else, just listen to me, okay Jenny? You do love me don't you, I don't know what I would do if you stopped loving me. I need you to be nice to me Jenny, no one else is you know. Okay honey? Promise me now."

I am still scared and confused. I tell him but he doesn't seem to hear me. His words are making me feel a little better but my stomach is still hurting. It's turning over inside as if I might throw up. I am trying to show him how crazy I feel and he can't understand. I am crying again and he is kissing each tear with his thick tongue. "No grandpa, please, I don't want to." I am silenced by his long, hard kiss on my open lips. His mouth is hard and slimy, bile is rising in my throat and I am suffocating. I am trying to push him away but he knows all too well I am vulnerable. He senses I still love him. still need him to rescue me from loneliness. By the time he leaves my room he has succeeded in cajoling me into promising I will not tell our secret. My own guilt and fears along with his overpowering need have made me vow never to tell anyone about the things he does to me.

Dec. 10, 1960

Dear Diary,

I have thirty-seven dollars saved, almost all of them are brand new. I can't think of anything to buy so I guess I'll Just keep hiding them in the box under my bed. If Debbie takes it I'll tell mama and if mama doesn't do anything I'll beat her up. I hate Debbie sometimes. She's such a grouch. Something real bad is wrong with my cousin Sonny. Something about his legs and stuff. He sure does fall down a lot. Aunt Lorraine said he's real sick but she wouldn't tell me what he has. Her and mama and grandma sit around the table talking about how awful it is all the time. Sonny says he doesn't know either but that when his dad comes home he will tell him. He just wishes he wouldn't keep falling down because he gets embarrassed in front of the other kids. I feel real sad about Sonny. I would trade places with him if I could. I think I might like to be sick, maybe even dying, then maybe I'd get lots of attention too.

Dec. 17, 1960

Dear Diary,

Great grandma Mary Elizabeth is coming home from the nursing home for Christmas. I like her and all because she taught me to read and stuff but she's so old and talks too much. Mama says she's real sick so I should be nice to her. I wish I were Grandma Mary. Debbie and mama got into a big fight last night because Jimmy and David get to do more than her and she always has to clean the house. When I grow up I'm going to be the best mama in the world. I'm going to have ten kids and spend all my time playing with them. I spent the night with Margie last night and she said I can live with them if I want. I'd like to but I know mama wouldn't let me. Sonny

*fell down five times today while we were playing war. Poor
Sonny, he cries a lot too.*

Dec. 23, 1960

Dear Diary,

*Yucky old Peter is back again. I think he's going to stay this
time. He is so creepy. I bought everyone their presents today.
I got a jar of sour balls for Grandma Sarah, a small book of
poems for Grandma Mary, five Hershey bars with almonds
for mama, an army tank for Sonny and a bunch of other stuff
for Debbie, Jimmy and David. Oh yeah, and a bottle of perfume for Aunt Lorraine. Were going to grandma's house for
Christmas dinner. Oh well. Mama doesn't care that I want to
stay home with just her. I hope mama buys me a Chatty Cathy
doll, that's all I really want except for a bike but mama says
I'll never get one from her because she's afraid I'll get run
over by a car. Who cares. Mama says I better start eating my
dinner and stop crying or she's going to take me to the doctor.
Yuk! She says I must be crazy to cry so much. Maybe she's
right.*

It was during the third grade that I became an expert at leading
a double life. The front I presented became my means of survival;
my way of coping with the conflict and guilt that raged so near
the surface. It's repulsiveness threatened to smother me. At
school and with my playmates I worked hard at being as I once
had been. Clear, concrete images of the carefree child ran
through my mind dictating my every movement. It was as
though a slow motion film played constantly before my eyes
molding me into the motions of childhood's freedom. Though I
was by no means as extroverted as I had been in the past I did

manage to find a compromise between the petrified and alienated person I had become and the open, friendly child of my past. The spontaneous Jennifer was dead and buried under the burden of intolerable pressure. I measured every word I said, every movement I made. Playing it all out before hand to make sure it fit with the role I had been cast in. My greatest fear, yet the one thing I longed for, was that someone, anyone, would suspect that there was something wrong with me. I dreamt of that moment, as though it would be suspended in time, over and over again; the ultimate second when someone would ask me the question I feared yet dreamed of with intensity and need.

I was locked away in the depths of a dark, cavernous dungeon filled with the filth of my own secrets and terror. I spent more and more time escaping into the safety of my books and my imaginary family. I now welcomed the early bedtime punishment, knowing it was my only way to leave the demands of my world and climb into the shelter of my illusions. I no longer tried to hide the evidence of my soiled bed from mama. In fact, there were many times I awoke right on the edge of wetting the bed and would choose to go ahead, knowing it meant a chance for a few moments of peace and quiet.

I became an imposter to myself and those who thought they knew me. My total self absorption kept me keenly aware of the figure I displayed to the world. This image soon became who "I was", as I became increasingly successful at separating from the real Jennifer. The natural actress within me bloomed in the role of "normal" child. I had become what mother always wanted to be, a star on a stage filled with outdated props and threadbare costumes.

Mother, mama. No longer did I follow her around the house, clutching at the hem of her flowered polyester dress, begging for her comfort and salvation. I had discovered and come to believe that she couldn't help me anymore than anyone else could. I knew that I would lose her love if she found out what happened between her father and me. I was alone with grandpa, there were no other alternatives. Because I needed her love so desperately I protected us both from her knowledge of our relationship. I believed and behaved as though my whole life was a secret. I even had trouble sharing the most simple information. Words caught in my throat with the consistency of half dried paste which I could neither swallow or spit out. So many, oh God, there were so very many seconds frozen in space when the screams battled for freedom of their own. Still I didn't, couldn't. I pushed them back down into the prison of my bloodied innocence where they churned and lunged, just barely within my control.

I kept myself hidden from everyone, especially Grandpa John. I barricaded myself with walls of superficiality, entrenched by the loss of realness. Oh sure, grandpa tried all his old tricks to gain my attention, attempting to seduce me with his humor and games. There again, caught in the middle. One part of me longing for the only caring available and the other nauseous at the mere sight of him. The war raged on within me.

The frequent escapes to my fantasy world produced such significant behavior changes in me that finally even mama noticed my altered state. She harped at me for appearing so tired, saying that I needed more sleep. She complained that I made her have more laundry to do because I started wearing two sets of underwear and extra pajamas at night. Tired of having to ask me everything at least twice she said maybe I needed my hearing checked. She only saw what she was able to see. She did not see the darkened fog that hovered over me, descending lower and lower. I yearned for mama to see what was there, for her to rescue me and make the hurt go away. Yet my own fear of her rejection and blame prevented me from reaching out to her. I loved her, I needed her, yet she never saw through the haze. I wondered how she could not see.

Feb. 26, 1961

Dear Diary,

We went to our new school today. It's really ugly, it looks like that big hospital Grandma Sarah was in last year. I don't know why they tore the other one down but I sure wish they hadn't. My new teacher is real creepy too. Her name is Mrs. Crowley and she's real old and fat. She always looks mad. She wears funny shoes with thick soles and seamed stockings that are always crooked. They kind of look like a winding road crawling up her calves. I wish I still had Miss Stevens, she was the best.

March 2, 1961

Dear Diary,

Grandma Mary Elizabeth is real sick. Mama says she might die. Mama got mad at me because I didn't cry when she told me. I won't miss going to the nursing home to visit her because it stunk like the inside of our laundry basket. We are studying geography in school, it's really neat. When I grow up I'm going to travel around the world and never come back to New York.

March 6, 1961

Dear Diary,

Sonny has some kind of disease in his legs, I think. No one will tell me anything but I heard Aunt Lorraine telling a friend that he's going to die. I've been real nice to him since then. I

*wish I could trade places with him or something. Grandma
Mary is getting sicker everyday and I still don't feel like crying. Mama says there's something wrong with me. I wonder.*

When Grandma Mary Elizabeth died mama sat all four of us
children down and instructed us that now was the time for tears.
Once again I knew that there was something very wrong with
me, so did mama, because I had no tears to shed for that old
woman. I didn't feel her death any more or any less than I felt
anything outside of myself. It was simply another act in an ongo-
ing drama. I read my script and attempted to act it out as best as
I knew how.

Mama insisted that her children attend the funeral to show
their respect for our great grandmother. For the two days prior to
the service I was panic stricken with anticipation. When the day
arrived I found myself seated in the family pew between Debbie
and Jimmy. The three of us were scared to death but Jimmy was
playing out his role of big brother in control. The open coffin
bearing Mary Elizabeth's eighty-year old body was directly in
front of us. I kept my eyes severely focused on one side of it. I
was in awe and amazed by the entire spectacle. I had never seen
a dead person before nor experienced so many people crying
and making horrible mourning sounds. The preacher went on to
mouth a mumble jumble of words about God and dying. He explained how Mary Elizabeth had gone to live in heaven with her
Almighty Father. I was so envious of her; the sounds of my own
prayers for death and life with God on the streets paved with
gold drowned out the voice of the southern preacher.

Somehow I got lost in my own fantasy and before I knew what
was happening people were lining up and filing past the open
coffin. Jimmy nudged me to take my place in the funeral proces-
sion but I had no desire to see that dead woman, grandmother or
not, and I tiptoed hesitantly behind Debbie. I was so scared that
I thought for sure I was going to wet my pants. I glanced up from

the darkly tiled floor to see mama and Aunt Lorraine looking into the large coffin and heard simultaneous blood curdling screams come from their collective mouths. That was all it took for me to run wildly out of the chapel leaving a trail of wetness on the smudgeless floor. Mama's best friend, Eunice ran after me and upon catching me held me locked in the warmth of her arms while I sobbed. I wasn't grieving about grandma's death as much as I was totally stricken by the shocking display of raw emotion in the little church.

While the rest of the family went on to the cemetery that afternoon, Eunice took her son and I to the park. I sat on the bottom of the slide, methodically licking an ice cream cone, thinking about all that I had heard and seen that morning. I decided then and there that if there was any possible way, I was going to join God above the clouds where everything was safe and wonderful.

Death and the idea of a secure life in heaven kept me brooding long after I had forgotten all about the death of Grandma Mary. I spent hours trying to figure out a way to die without it hurting too much. Many afternoons I sat under the fading sun, my feet dangling in the gutter, imagining myself being crushed by the oncoming traffic. I spent even more time visualizing the funeral service my mother would have for me where everyone would cry about how badly they had treated me. I imagined my grandfather standing off to the side, for the first and only time not being more important to mama than I was. Sometimes I pretended I would come back to life, and give them all a second chance to treat me the way they should. I had discovered that there was a way out of being who I was and living the way I did. The lure of death and the peace of the afterlife was to become a form of security for me for many years to come.

As the third grade year came to a close, I became more and more frightened of the craziness living within me. Sometimes I couldn't tell if the act was me or I was the act. I so needed to feel normal and wanted, yet the only person who had time for me was Grandpa John.

I wanted grandpa to hold me and make me feel safe but whenever I allowed myself to give into our need for one another I felt confused and guilty. The more I fought my love for him, and his obvious need for me, the more confused I became. The worst part of all was the torment of the secret we shared. I desperately wanted to tell someone what he was doing to me and have them make it stop but I was still driven to him for love and consolation. An intuitive part of me knew that the intimacy between my grandfather and I was wrong. Another part wholeheartedly believed him when he said it was normal and good. I needed to believe him in order to continue receiving his love. Whenever I told him of my concerns he made it clear that I was just a child and therefore my feelings were invalid. He said he knew better than I did. Between his oppressive need for me and my growing suspicion, I was being torn apart.

I knew the secrets we agreed to keep from everyone had to remain hidden and he continually made me promise to keep them. Still there were times when it almost came spurting out of my mouth like an uncontrollable volcanic eruption. But I had to keep my oath to him above all else. Otherwise I would lose the only love I knew. Because I was forbidden to tell anyone about our relationship I was forced to be even more intimate with him by confiding my deepest fears. Though I had no name for what he did to me and was mostly unable to verbalize my feelings, sometimes I felt like I would explode unless I screamed out some of the confusion I felt. I was totally alone and isolated and there seemed to be no one to turn to except Grandpa John. He had all the control and I did whatever he ordered. When I did gather up the courage to talk about it at all, I only ended up even more confused. He always said the same things in response to my pleas for answers and clarity.

"No, no little Jen, there's nothing wrong with the way I love you. You're so special, how could I ever do anything to hurt you?" His hypnotic voice both frightened and captured me. I was powerless under his spell.

"But grandpa why can't I tell anyone and why do I feel so bad sometimes?" I pleaded with him.

"This is our special secret, honey, no one else would understand", he replied. "You promised you wouldn't say anything. Besides, it might hurt your grandma, to know, how much I love you. There's nothing wrong with what we're doing. It feels good doesn't it? Now promise me you won't say a word. Come on, be grandpa's little girl and tell me you won't say anything, okay?"

"But grandpa, I'm scared. I don't like it. I just want you to hug me. I don't want you to do that other stuff anymore," I begged.

"I love you Jen, how many times do I have to tell you that! My touching you is part of my loving you. Now come here and be a good girl. Give grandpa a big kiss," he demanded.

I went along with him for a while, accepting what he preached. I had to believe him since he gave me the love I craved. And yet as much as I wanted him to stop touching me I couldn't stay away from him. Sometimes I even felt a sense of comfort from his repetitious explanations and for a short while was able to go about pretending there was nothing wrong with me. Then, out of nowhere, I would remember something or hear something new, and once again do battle between what was right and wrong. I believed I was crazy. I was terrified that someone would lock me up if they ever found out.

May 3, 1961

Dear Diary,

Mama is mad at me again, she says I'm too skinny and had better eat more or else she'll take me to the doctor. Mama says my body is changing and soon I will be a woman. I'm not sure what she means but that's the last thing I want to be. I wish I could be a baby again and daddy could feed me and play with me and stuff. The thing I wish for most is that my daddy would come home. Then everything would be fine. Mama says Peter is my daddy now and that I must love him. Yuk!

May 10, 1961

Dear Diary,

Mama asked me if I wanted to have a party for my ninth birthday but I said no. She said there's something very wrong with me, that I don't act like other little girls. Debbie wants to have a party for her birthday but mama said she is too old. Jimmy is trying to talk mama into letting him join the Army. Mama gets real mad when he brings it up. David has a girlfriend and boy is she ugly. Mitzi is going to have puppies soon and I want one for my birthday. Mama said maybe.

May 28, 1960

Dear Diary,

Tomorrow is my birthday and mama said I can have my pick of the puppies. I like the ugly white one, I'm going to name him Mr. Wiggins after a movie I saw the other day. I'm not going to camp this year and I'm sure glad. Mama and Peter are fighting a lot again, he threw a cigarette at her last night, he is so weird.

Our house. I guess it was just about like everyone else's on our block. A conventional three story row house with a brick lined basement and a small yard extending out to a narrow alley brimming with trash cans. The living room was on the ground floor along with a kitchen and bath. The living room and kitchen opened up into each other making both rooms appear much larger than they actually were. My bedroom was on the second floor along with mama and Peter's and another bath. My room was the smallest one in the house. There was barely enough space to crowd a bunk bed, tiny dresser and night stand. The best part of my room was the fire escape and window over looking the busy street below. I had a clear view of all that happened below me on Columbus Avenue and spent many hours watching the neighbors live out their lives. Debbie, Jimmy, and David shared the rooms on the top level of the house.

Grandpa John babysat for me on the evenings when everyone else was gone. Debbie had recently been hired to work behind the candy counter at a movie house in the neighborhood. Jimmy and David were usually hanging out on one street corner or another and mama was helping grandma in the dark room down the street so grandpa and I were thrown together because of our uselessness to anyone else. When I was younger I enjoyed it when grandpa came to take care of me because he would play games and hold me while we watched TV. However as his sexual advances heightened I became increasingly fearful of those nights alone with him. Some evenings, however, were like old times; we played cards and shared laughter about purely nonsensical things.

That was one of the hardest, most confusing things about grandpa; I just never knew what he might do, one minute he was funny and playful and the next he was melancholy and demanding. It was the other nights that scared me so, the times I knew for sure that grandpa wanted more than just an audience for his jokes.

I am lying on the floor, the softness of the thick carpet being twirled between my fingers is gently ticklish. I am wearing two pairs of pajamas on top of three tee shirts and four pairs of underwear, the layers of elastic are cutting into my thighs; I must pull them up constantly, the chafing is itchy and raw. Lucy is before me dressed in Italian peasant clothing and dancing in a large tub of grapes. She is fighting with another woman, they are both covered with oozing grape juice from head to toe. I am totally engrossed in the hilarious grape battle except for the one hand that is tugging on the bothersome underwear. From a million miles away I hear someone or something moving about, it is as though wads of old newspaper are being rustled.

"Come here Jen, come sit with me on the couch," his words sneak through and the rustling noise ends abruptly. My heart is pounding so loudly it is drowning out the sound of Lucy's laughter. My throat constricts in fear. My breathing is shallow but so noisy that it is though my heart and breath are playing a raucous duet.

"No. No go away, I want to watch Lucy, leave me alone." No words can be heard through the uproar of my mind.

"Jenny, I'm talking to you, come here and sit with me right now."

I raise my voice, the words gushing out in torrents to pierce the moment. "I don't want to grandpa, I like it here on the floor."

"Turn off the television and come over here right now if you know what's good for you." His own voice is a cacophony of expectation.

"But grandpa I'm watching Lucy, it's my favorite show, please can't I watch it, huh?" I am trying. so hard to seduce him with my sweetness.

"I'll make a deal with you. You can watch it but only if you sit with me, otherwise just turn the damned thing off. Understand?"

Slowly, so reluctantly, I lift myself up on legs that feel like Jello before it sets. My stomach is burning, little tastes of bile filling my mouth as I cross the room to do as I am ordered and take my rightful place next to him. Grandpa is putting one arm around me and nuzzling the back of my neck. His breath is hot and sticky smelling. I sit, stiff and straight, my back arched tightly against the cushions, my arms straining around my chest, my knees crunched together as one. I am staring at the TV intently trying to make Lucy the only one in the room. His hands are so insistent with their demands. He is kissing my neck; leaving wet, slobbery trails behind. One large paw running down my chest. I am trying so hard to pretend he isn't real, isn't here now tracing circles on the mound of my stomach. I am concentrating on Lucy, silly old Lucy as she tries to manipulate Ricky once again, but it is so difficult to maintain the vision of her humor as his hands reach down to the target he seeks.

"I love you Jen," his whispers competing with Lucy's howling. "I don't feel so good, I need you to take care of me baby," he is oozing at me, clueing me in to what he wants.

"No grandpa, I don't want to. I don't feel like being nice to you, oh please grandpa, can't I just watch TV Please, huh, please can't I watch this?" I am begging again, my voice whiny and constricted, arising from my aching chest.

"Don't give me any crap girl, you just sit there and be the good little girl that you know you better be."

His fingers are probing, pushing my thighs apart roughly. I give in, there is nothing else to do. I melt into the television set and join Lucy and Ricky's world. The heavy thudding in my ears grows louder and louder deadening the sound of grandpa's raspy breathing and low moans. The grate of his zipper intrudes violently. I am floating along on a cloud high above the scene on the couch, I can see that girl with the heavy hair covering her face, there are streams of tears pouring from her closed eyes. She is as still as death's sleep. The only movement is the old man's hand on himself. He is crying out words that make no sense from my place up here. Jerkily he jumps up pulling his pants up haphazardly around his waist. Still the girl sits there suffocating in her own pain. He is yelling at her to move, to get out of his sight. Still nothing, not even a slight movement of an involuntary muscle. Louder and louder his words hang above her. She hears none of it. He reaches out shaking her thin shoulders wildly and still she sees and hears nothing. Her futile layers of protection lie dangling around her ankles, she is clutching each arm with fingernails ground through the cloth. He is lifting her up, carelessly tugging her pajamas back to where they belong. Screams coming from his mouth, words her mother would cringe at. He is carrying her up the stairs, I follow on my cloud to see him throw her onto the bottom bunk. Still the girl says and does nothing as the tears are gushing from their prison doors.

June 5, 1961

Dear Diary,

Mama told me this morning that I will be going to camp again with the Peterson's. I'm not sure how I feel about that, I think I'd like it if I were going to be the only kid there. At least Debbie isn't going this year. Maybe Sally and Connie won't be there either. I hope not. Mrs. Crowley sent a note home to mama saying she was concerned about my performance in school. Mama got mad again and said I'd better straighten up. My grades are all A's but Mrs. Crowley says I don't participate anymore. Mama said little girls aren't supposed to stay off by themselves. Mama also said I've been acting weird, she said I'd better start being normal or else.

June 10, 1961

Dear Diary,

I just finished reading the Little Prince, it is the most wonderful book ever. I feel like he did sometimes, kind of lonely and out of place. Things are so weird around here, no one is talking to each other, which is okay with me but mama gets so upset. Jimmy and David got into some kind of trouble with the police and mama and grandma had to bail them out. Mama cried a lot and Jimmy just kept begging her to let him join, the army. David is just a creep, he thinks he's so hot. I can't stand him or Debbie. I have fifty-six dollars saved now.

The sexual relationship between my grandfather and I had by now escalated to the point of almost weekly encounters, sometimes more. In between these nightmarish sessions I tried to wipe them out of my mind. I pretended that Grandpa John was still only a kind old man with funny stories and a big heart. I felt so empty inside. Sometimes I likened myself to those chocolate bunnies mama gave me for Easter. They are a rich dark chocolate on the outside with pink candy eyes and mouth but when you bite into them they are deceptively hollow. They are so pretty to look at but inside there's nothing but emptiness and dark corners to hide secrets.

Grandpa still showed up in my room in the darkness of night on occasion but when he did he seemed panicky and hurried and made limited sexual overtures. I slept poorly now, it was as though each night I lay in waiting, never knowing if tonight would be another one of those nights or not. It was the daytime meetings that were the foundation of my nightmares, the times we were alone at his house or mine. Though grandpa usually began his molestation in a similar manner by cleverly entrapping me within the folds of gentleness and power, he slowly began introducing new dimensions into our relationship.

There she is again, sitting so close, his paternal arm engulfing her thin frame. Her glazed eyes are narrowly focused on me, lying up here, a darkened rain spot left to dry on a cracking plaster ceiling. She sees me and nothing else, I am smiling down to her trying to encourage her journey to my space. He is shaking her shoulders roughly, yelling Jenny! Jenny! in that gravely angry tone he has assumed lately. She sits tightly, awkwardly entwined in her own world, she does not see or hear him.

"God damn it, Jennifer listen to me!" he is slapping her face, a bright hand print lingers to smolder on her delicate face. Still no response from the girl, her eyes cloud over heavily.

Aha, a new approach, he is whispering now, his voice oozing and flowing around her hypnotically. "Jenny honey, please baby talk to me, I love you so much, Jenny talk to me!" One arm twitches sending it flailing without purpose against his chest. "Jenny, you don't want to make grandpa mad, now do you. There's no reason I have to get mad at you girl, but if you keep this up I swear to God your going to make me do something I don't want to. And you'll have no one to blame except yourself little girl, understand?" He is lighting a cigarette, its flame bright and hot as he is leaning in, so close, whispering again so softly that even I cannot hear his pleas. He lifts her top, she is wearing triple layers of futility. His cigarette dangles from his yellowed fingertips, hovering tenuously over the space between her tiny nipples. He is looking into her vacant eyes. Slowly he lowers the ember tip searing the surface of her transparent skin. Screams, wild animal sounding screeches from the girl on the flowered couch, her eyes torn from my protection.

"Didn't I warn you girl? I told you to knock off the baloney and talk to me. It's your own fault that I had to hurt you. Now quit your bellyaching, there's hardly even a mark there. Quit screaming like that Jenny. You better shut up right now." I cannot even see him as my eyes overflow with pain. "Come on baby please just quiet down. If you be a good little girl I'll give you the surprise I have in my pocket, okay baby?" I am bursting with hatred yet here I sit mummified against the cushion. "Jenny please, come on now, I have two brand new dollar bills for you, just quit your crying and I'll give them to you, okay now, come on."

My words are low, moaned rather than spoken, "I hate you."

Grandpa is not looking, at me, he is thumping his knee with restless fingers. The moment feels like it is waiting for reprieve,

The only sound is the tick-tock, tick-tock of the clock in the oppressive silence. We sit here mirror images of each other, our arms clinging to our shared anguish, our eyes fixated on minute particles of dust flying through the thickened air. Seconds creep by in mute uproar. Neither of us are moving, the only way I can be sure I am alive is by the slight sensation of air being pulled into expanded lungs.

Minutes or hours or perhaps even days later I am given my next directive, "Get out of my sight Jenny, I can't stand this anymore."

June 30, 1961

Dear Diary,

In two days I am leaving for camp. I'm really glad to going away from here for two months. Lately I hate New York, it is such an ugly, scary city. Mama bought me four new short sets and a pair of sandals. She even remembered to buy insect repellant. Since school let out a week ago I have read four books, my favorite series of books are by Beverly Cleary. I wish I were Ramona. I have decided that when I grow up I will either be an actress or a writer. Either one of those jobs will earn me good money and then I can move away from here. Jimmy and mama have been fighting everyday for two weeks. I think mama is

just about to give in and let him join the Army. He is seven-
teen now and mama can't do anything about stopping him
anyhow. Jimmy and David have been arguing a lot too. David
wants to go with Jimmy but there is no way mama will let
them both leave. Debbie seems to be much happier now that she
is working most every evening. Next year when I enter the
fourth grade I will start cooking and sewing lessons. I think
I'm going to like that. Mama gave me five dollars for my report
card. She yelled a little about the comments Mrs. Crowley
wrote about my not participating in classroom discussions,
but overall I think she was pleased.

Someone is calling my name, the sound of the word Jenny is
stretched out and muffled by clouds of sleepiness. I am running
through a long dark tunnel. I am not sure whether I am running
away from the words or towards them, they are dancing about
me, bouncing off the narrow walls of the opaque passageway.
The strong taste of sour bile catches in my throat chocking back
the growing terror.

"Jenny. Jenny. Wake up sweet Jenny." The voice is stronger,
clearer now. "Come on Jenny, wake up for grandpa." The darkened tunnel opens up into my bedroom, the only light is the
burning ash on the tip of grandpa's cigarette as it dangles awkwardly between his slightly parted lips. Though I can't see his
face I know it is him, the strength of his Old Spice surrounds me.
I close my eyes, pretending I am still captured by the shelter of
sleep. "Come on now Jenny, I know you're awake. Don't play
possum with me little girl." I don't dare move. I am holding my
breath, my cheeks puffed out like a chipmunk harvesting his
winter's store. He is shaking me gently. "Jen, please Jen, just talk
to me for a minute. I feel so lonely. I need you."

I roll over to the wall, pleading with it to take me within its
shelter. I am clutching the woolen blankets around my shoulders, imagining them to be layers of steel. His hand is rubbing

my back while his soft spoken words hypnotize me to the spot. "Oh Jenny honey, please talk with me. I really need you to be nice to me tonight...You're the only one who's ever nice to me. Please Jenny."

The voice that erupts from my throat is gravelly and harsh, "Turn on the light, I hate this darkness."

Grandpa gets up, turns on the light in the hall, closes the door half-way and returns to his place on the edge of my bed. "Is that better honey? Now will you talk to me?"

"I don't want to talk to you, I don't even want to see you. Why can't you just leave me alone. I want to sleep."

"But Jenny I need you. If you just let me touch you for awhile I'll go away and you can get back to sleep. Is that a deal kiddo?"

"What difference does it make if it is or not? You'll do what you want anyway."

"I don't like your attitude little girl. I never do anything to you that you don't want me to and you know it." I hear the change in his tone, I know that if I do not behave as he wants he will only get angry.

"Sure grandpa, whatever you say." The sarcasm in my voice is clear but he chooses to ignore it. He reaches out to me, lifting me into his arms. Sitting on his lap I feel the hardness of his thing against my bottom. His hands travel across my chest under the layers of clothing meant to be a barrier. His guttural whispers whisk past my ears, all I hear are the mumbles of his needs. He is placing me back on the wrinkled sheets, pulling my pants down to my knees. The roar of his zipper being undone pushes me towards escape. He is shaking me again, this time roughly, against the wall.

"Jenny God damn it, don't pull that pretending you're not here game on me. I need you right here with me, I want to teach you something new. Hear me girl?

There is no need for me to answer. I lay there mutely with my hands braced against the bed.

"Look at me honey, I have something wonderful for you." He is holding his white, worm like appendage in his right hand. I turn away afraid and disgusted. He has never made me look at his ugliness before. Even when he forced my hand over it I hadn't actually looked at it. He is turning my head in his direction, crooning empty words of persuasion. "Jenny baby, it needs you. It needs you to kiss it and make it feel better." He is balancing his body over my face, the stench of urine causes me to cough. My stomach is in spasms, vomit rises in my throat.

"I'm going to be sick." my words are flat and weightless. My eyes are shut tightly, white bugs are dancing in the blackness of my lids.

"Don't worry honey, you'll be just fine. This will make you feel really good." His penis is brushing against my clenched mouth, the soft hardness being forced between my teeth. "Open up Jenny. Don't make me mad, I'm warning you, do as you're told."

Tears, warm and gushing down my shuttered eyes. I am drowning in my fear. He is moving away from me, the bed groans in relief. "Alright, alright honey, let's just try something different. I promise you're going to like this. Come here now, come and sit near me." He peels me off the sheet, pushing me into a sitting position facing him on the bed. "Please Jenny, just try this once, okay? I'll do anything you say or give you anything you want, okay? Huh honey, please just for me." Still I say nothing, I am locked into an upright fetal position, my arms locked around my rib cage. He is pulling my hair, inching my mouth down to his exposed body. My heart is thumping loudly against my chest, tears land in circular puddles on his penis.

"No, no, please grandpa, don't make me do that. I can't stand it, please, I'll do anything but don't make me do that. I'll throw up, I know I will. Oh God I feel so sick."

"Jenny, you know I wouldn't do anything to hurt you. Just try it, okay, and if you don't like it you can stop." Both of his large hands are holding my head in place on top of him, He is pleading with me to take him inside my mouth. My lips are locked together, I cannot make them budge. "Jenny open up your mouth, God dammit! Do it now girl because you're starting to make me really mad. Remember last time you made me hurt you? I don't want to have to do that again. now do I?"

"His penis feels like stiffened spaghetti against my closed lips, urine and sweat bring on new waves of nausea.

"No grandpa, please don't. You might pee on me or something.

"Don't be silly I can't pee on you. Now go on girl put it in your mouth."

I am trying to push my body away from his grip. he only holds on tighter, grinding my face into his crotch. I am trying to do what he wants. He is scaring me. I'm so afraid he will hurt me again. I feel its wrinkled flesh against the roof of my mouth. Oh God, it is growing, I cough and spit him out.

"Do it Jenny, put it back in, suck it really gentle like. Go on, put it into your mouth. I know you're going to be real good at this. You're such a Good little girl. Grandpa's favorite you know. Oh yeah, I love you so much." I know nothing but the humiliation of the thing swelling in my half open mouth.

She is there below me, she doesn't see me but I see her clearly. Her head is bent over, his fingers digging into her tangled hair. His face is lifted towards me but he can't see me either. His eyes are closed, his mouth gaping open. She is choking on her sobs, his pants are wet with her tears. Time is marked off slowly by the sound of strained breathing and muffled cries.

He is leaving now. Gathering up his clothes around him. He covers up the deadened child gently with sheets and blankets before walking, head hung low, through the door of a once darkened tunnel. She lays there, in a daze, eyes piercing through me, on the ceiling above. She is crying but there are no words for her pain. Time passes slowly filling in the empty spaces around her. She cries softly down the stairs, past Grandpa John as he sits on the couch watching television, into the bathroom, where she sits on the edge of the tub, watching the steam rise from the hot water pouring in. Her tears blend with the soapy water as she scrubs herself raw.

July 10, 1961

Dear Diary,

I've been at camp for two weeks now. So far it's been pretty boring. Sally and Connie are here again but I don't like them much anymore. They both have boyfriends now and all they talk about are boys, boys and more boys. There is a new boy here this year, his name is Richard and he is a real creep. He's always looking at me funny. Aunt Susan has been griping at me all the time. She says I don't eat enough to keep a bird alive and that I shouldn't spend so much time off by myself. She says it isn't healthy. I don't see what's so bad a about wanting to be alone but she says it isn't normal. Connie calls me stuck-up and says she doesn't want to be around me because I'm a drag. I don't really care what she or anyone else thinks. I just wish they'd mind their own business and leave me alone. There's nothing wrong with me, I'm just fine, right?

July 15, 1961

Dear Diary,

My body is starting to do strange things. My chest is changing and I don't like it at all. My nipples seem to be getting bigger, yuk! I think I'm getting fat too, because my pants are becoming too tight around my hips, but the weird part is that they are looser around my waist. I don't know what's going on but I sure wish it would go away. I've noticed that Sally and Connie look different this year too, but they're older than me. I sure do wish I was a boy then I wouldn't have to worry about any of this junk.

Aug. 6, 1961

Dear Diary,

I've been on a diet and I've lost almost five pounds but still my chest keeps getting bigger. This morning I stood in front of the bathroom mirror and tried to push my nipples into my chest with my thumbs but they wouldn't go. I am so ugly and so darn fat even though I haven't been eating much at all. Aunt Susan is jumping all over me again. She says I will waste away to nothing. Aunt Susan talked to all us girls about how we should be proud of our changing bodies because it means we're becoming women. When she talks about that stuff I feel like screaming, but I don't. I just sit there staring at the disgusting plate full of soggy food and nod my head. She's also been teasing me lately because Richard is always trying to hang around me. He follows me all over the place and even when I ignore him or tell him to get lost he just stands there and makes googoo eyes at me. He makes me sick and even a little bit scared. Aunt Susan says he has a crush on me and I should be flattered but I think it's creepy. I hate boys. When I grow up I'm never getting married.

Aug. 13, 1961

Dear Diary,

I got a letter from mama today. She wrote that Jimmy is going to join the Army and is leaving for North Carolina next month. I feel kind of sad about him going away because he's really the only one in my family that is half way nice to me. I guess it doesn't really matter that much because he can't make things different than they are anyway. I found a complete set of Nancy Drew books out in the shed and have read five of them already. She seems to have a great family. Sometimes I can't get to sleep and I pretend I'm her living with my 'real' family.

Aug. 20, 1961

Dear Diary,

A couple of days ago I found the ugliest black hair on my private parts. I used Mr. Peterson's razor to shave it. off but now there are two. I'm going to keep shaving them off because hair down there is really nasty. I've lost nine pounds now but I still look fat. Whenever Aunt Susan sees me on the scale she comes running over like I'm breaking some law or something. She keeps asking how much weight I've lost and how much I weigh. I told her I'd only lost four pounds, she seems less upset with me since then, but she still picks on me to eat more. She has been threatening to tell mama about my bad behavior as she calls it. Mama won't care anyway so it's no big deal.

Aug. 25, 1961

Dear Diary,

I wrote to Jimmy and asked him to take me with him to North Carolina. I doubt that he'll say yes, it's probably not even allowed, but I sure would like to go. Sally and Connie are being so mean lately. They call me string bean and say I'm crazy because I wake them up screaming in the middle of the night. Aunt Susan said that from now on I have to sleep on a cot in the living room, with the light on, so that I won't wake them up from their precious sleep. I'm glad I can sleep out there, at least now I won't have to listen to their boy-talk all night. Richard keeps bugging me too. Now he's writing me love letters as well as chasing me around the cottage. He makes me want to throw up.

Sept. 3, 1961

Dear Diary,

Mama is coming to pick me up tomorrow. I wish I could just stay here especially now that everyone else has gone home already. I don't ever want to go back to New York. I hate it there. I'm going to ask mama if I can go away to boarding school. I think she might say yes because I'm such a bother to her anyway. I can even use my own money to go because I have eighty-one dollars saved now. I've lost thirteen pounds now and nothing fits anymore but my chest is still growing. Aunt Susan says I will need a bra soon. I'll never wear one of those ugly things. I wish I could figure out a way to not have to go back there with her, but there's no where else to go.

Sept. 13, 1961

Dear Diary,

I started school today and it's even worse than last year. My new teacher is just like Miss Crowley except she's even older and uglier though not quite as mean. The fourth grade is supposed to be different but this seemed just as babyish as last year. Margie is in my class again but she doesn't like me anymore. It feels like nc one really likes me but I don't care, Who needs them anyway. Last night we has dinner at grandma Sarah's house and Sonny fell down at least twenty times while we were playing. I heard mama and Aunt Lorraine say he is getting sicker all the time. We stayed away from the grown-ups. I don't think he likes them any better than I do, though we didn't actually talk about it.

Sept. 17, 1961

Dear Diary,

I took my new book, Alice in Wonderland, to share at school today and creepy old Joe Corrotolli wrote I want to fuck you in it. He makes me so sick, I wish he were dead. If mama sees it she'll get so mad at me. She thinks everything is my fault. Tomorrow night we are having a big dinner for Jimmy. He is leaving for the Army on Saturday. I don't want him to go but he says he has to. I don't understand at all. I think he just wants to get away from mama. His girlfriends have been coming over and crying all the time. Mama cries a lot too, I bet she wouldn't cry if I went away. I sure wish I was old enough to join the army.

In my grandparent's home there was a basement that served several purposes for the family. The room was set up as a darkroom where mama worked evenings and weekends developing and printing film for John and Sarah's photography studio. On the rare occasions when mama let me watch her make pictures from dark negatives I was totally enchanted. The basement also served as a storage area for objects that were no longer needed or used. Sometimes while mama worked I would rummage through the boxes to find wonderful old and fascinating surprises.

There was also a bathroom with an old battered toilet. This toilet was the scene of many of my most horror-filled nightmares. Whenever I was forced to choose between wetting my pants and mama's certain disapproval or giving into the monsters of the basement toilet it never failed to be an agonizing decision. My wild imagination created the most terrifying visions about the old toilet. I was positive there were huge rats with red bulging eyes that came up from the bowels of the earth to bite me on the butt. I also believed there were giant snakes slinking in the bottom of the stained bowl that would hiss and strike with their cruel tongues and cause instant death. I hated that toilet and though I always escaped an early death I was convinced it would happen the very next time my thin rear end was placed upon its seat. I tried to avoid making contact with the toilet seat by hovering above it, but I often missed the bowl completely. My exaggerated fear of this bathroom soon became a family joke. My brothers and sister never missed a chance to increase my terror by telling me they had actually seen a rat or snake down there, just waiting for me.

The basement was also where my grandfather dealt out mama's punishments for her children. Grandpa John had long been the one responsible for spanking us when the need arose. On such occasions grandpa would lead us down the narrow stairs and whip us with his wide leather belt on the small day bed placed their for that purpose. Since Jimmy and David were nearly grown they rarely had to go down in the basement with grandpa anymore. Debbie would brag after one of her trips downstairs that grandpa never really whipped her anyhow. Her story was that he pretended to spank her while he really just walloped the bed and she screamed loudly to satisfy mama. She would be right upstairs, sitting around the kitchen table with grandma, listening for the sounds of a howling child.

For me the story was quite different. The few times I was ordered down the stairs with Grandpa John were most unpleasant. He either really did spank me or he used these golden opportunities to molest me. Either way I was instructed to pull my pants down and lie on the day bed. I was told to lie on my stomach if a spanking was in order and on my back if he was planning on being sexual with me. When I was younger I had given into his wishes immediately, knowing that I was about to receive the punishment that mama had warned me about. Now that the spankings were less frequent my resistance to his demands grew stronger. I argued with him loudly before accepting my fate and giving in. Then I would lie there on my back, with my arms wound tightly around me staring at a spot on the ceiling or with my eyes shut tight trying to imagine the safety of my fantasy world. He sat on the edge of the bed staring at my naked lower half while he touched himself. Sometimes he would feel me with his other hand, usually not. I endured these assaults on my mind and, body as I did every other sexual contact with him now. I tried to be invisible and pretend it wasn't happening. When he was done he would wash himself at the small sink, tell me to get upstairs and sit on the corner of the bed, eyes focused on the cement floor while I went upstairs to mama. As I walked through the kitchen door mama would abruptly stop whatever conversation she was involved in. "Now, Jenny, just remember to be a good girl and grandpa won't have to do that anymore, understand? I don't like to have to punish you anymore than you do but you have to learn to obey me and behave yourself. Do you hear me Jennifer?"

These sexual encounters occurred while mama and grandma were upstairs, right above me. I thought about telling them what was going on down there but I never did. I kept my promise devoutly. Since she was the one who sent me down there, I believed that she had somehow approved the whole thing. No one cared about what happened to me when I was alone with grandpa.

Oct. 27, 1961

Dear Diary,

I'm not going to dress up for Halloween this year. I'm much too old and it's stupid anyway. Besides I don't really have anyone to go with and mama won't let me go alone. So far this year I have earned all A's in school. Mama gave me five dollars for my report card and said I'm the smartest girl she knows. David only got three dollars and Debbie didn't get any. I like it that I'm smarter than they are It's about the only thing that I'm any good at. I have ninety-four dollars saved now. Soon

I'll have enough to pay for boarding school. Maybe then mama will let me go because she said she couldn't afford it. Grandma Sarah is sick again and has to stay In bed all the time. Sometimes I go down there and pretend I'm her nurse, but not very often.

Nov. 2, 1961

Dear Diary,

Mama and Peter have been fighting again. Last night I woke up in the middle of the night to the sounds of them screaming at each other. I got up and sat at the top of the stairs and heard mama tell him he would have to leave unless things changed right away. I sure hope he goes. Maybe then life will be better around here, though I really doubt it.

He is such a nothing here, no one pays much attention to him. I heard him tell mama that she loves her parents more than him. I think he's right. Sonny is going to the hospital tomorrow for some kind of test on his legs. He's scared about it all, I wish I could go for him. I think I'd like to be in the hospital and have people bring me candy and toys.

My family's involvement with the local Baptist church had always been a major part of my life and I now became even more caught up with the teachings of Christianity. Mama was a Sunday school teacher and Grandpa John was an usher so we were all supposed to attend Sunday morning and evening services as well as prayer meeting on Wednesday night. However, Jimmy and David were often excused from this religious routine. Mama met such resistance from them that she usually let them do as they pleased which was anything other than go to church. For

Debbie and me there was absolutely no choice but regular atten-
dance. I used this religious requirement as another means to escape the problems at home as well as try to understand why God
had decided I should be so unhappy. I listened closely to the ser-
mons and read the bible daily, always searching for clues to why
I had the. kind of life I did. I found few answers but I tried to read
between the lines to see what God could do about the things
Grandpa John did to me. I prayed to Jesus nightly and believed
that if he chose to he could heal all of my hurts and turn me into
a happy child again. I begged God's forgiveness of my many sins
and even went so far to join the church and be baptized. I hoped
this symbol would somehow cleanse me of the filth of grandpa's
touch.

One Sunday, a missionary from Africa spoke to the congregation about her work in the jungle, trying to save the natives
from hell. I made a deal with God that same evening that if he
would make grandpa leave me alone I would make up for all the
badness by being a missionary when I grew up. While I still
imagined death as a way out of the craziness I felt, the idea
frightened more than comforted me. The preacher often spoke of
sinners burning in hell forever and I was afraid I would end up
there instead of in the glorified heaven. I knew I had sinned, that
I was a bad person and I greatly feared the wrathful God I heard
about each week. I was determined to be absolutely perfect so
that Jesus would forgive me and take me to his home in heaven.
I believed that was the only place I could ever be safe from
grandpa.

I was totally infatuated with one woman in our congregation.
Her name was Lois and I named my most favorite dolls after her.
I thought she was a heavenly angel sent by God himself. She was
tall and darkly beautiful with shiny black hair that flowed over
her shoulders and deep blue eyes. She spoke softly and smiled
frequently. I idolized her and used her as my personal role
model. I dreamt of her taking me home to live with her. I believed she would be as perfect as my imaginary family. She
seemed to like me too as she often stopped to say hello and ask
how I was doing. I followed her all around the church. Whenever
there was the slightest opportunity, I sat near her and stared

longingly at her lovely face. If I had the chance to actually touch her I walked around on a cloud for hours. I believe she was my first childhood crush.

School still played a major role in my life. At least there I felt somewhat safe, although always very different from the rest of my classmates. I especially enjoyed learning about faraway countries. We spent a month studying England and I easily took what I learned and used it in my nightly fantasy trips. I imagined my "real" family and I taking a cruise to London and seeing all the famous sights. I was still an excellent student and received much attention for my achievements. It was easy for me to be good at school work, it was clear and uncomplicated and I could do it alone. Also, the teachers wanted no more than what I already was, bright and creative. They praised me for that consistently. Although I was still one of the smartest children in class I was no longer a very social child. I was secretive and distant with both teachers and classmates. I no longer volunteered to share my ideas with the class. More and more I stayed off by myself, spending free time caught up in my own private world.

I wasn't much fun anymore and few of the kids in class or in my neighborhood wanted to play with me. I spent most of my time reading books on the fire escape or walking through the streets with my head hung low. I was totally preoccupied with what was going on between my grandfather and me. He was now molesting me at least once a week.

Jan 5, 1962

Dear Diary,

Uncle Danny has been transferred to the Navy base in Long Beach, California. He and Aunt Lorraine and Sonny are moving next month. Grandma Sarah and mama are trying to decide whether we should move there since they need to help out with Sonny. Jimmy is also in California now and mama wants

decide whether we should move there since they need to help
out with Sonny. Jimmy is also in California now and mama
wants us to be all together again. Except for Peter, thank God.
He moved out before Christmas and mama says he's never
coming back. I think I would like to live out west. They say
there's always sunshine and lots of things to do. Maybe then
we can live farther away form Grandma Sarah and everything.

Jan. 10, 1962

Dear Diary,

Mama has decided we are moving to California in June. I think
I'm happy about it. Mama says everything will be wonderful
once we are all together again. I hope she's right. Debbie and
David are so lucky. They get to move out there with Uncle
Danny and Aunt Lorraine in two weeks. I wish I could go but
mama says she needs me here with her. At least I will get to live
alone with her. Maybe things will be alright after all. Grandma
said that California is the place where everything is possible, I
hope she's right. I've decided that I want to be a movie star
when I grow up and being in California should make that
easier. I'm glad to be leaving here. I hate New York and I'm
never coming back here as long as I live.

One evening shortly after David and Debbie left for Long
Beach, while mama and I sat at the now too large dinner table,
she announced that we were going to move in with my
grandparents. I stared at her with wide eyes brimming with tears
as she went on to explain. "Jenny, we neither need nor can afford
to stay in this big house now that everyone else is gone. I need to
save a lot of money before we can move and I can't do that stay-

ing here. Besides it will be fun to live with ma and daddy again, don't you think?"

I couldn't believe what she was saying. My mouth refused to move. I stared at her, mouth gaping open with green beans hanging out and eyes that bored holes in her.

"What in the world is wrong with you Jen? Close your mouth. It looks disgusting. Don't you want to live with grandma and grandpa? I think it will be real nice for all of us. It will sure make babysitting easier on me. Jennifer quit looking at me like that, say something."

Tears fell from my eyes, landing in the cold pile of mashed potatoes. The food in my mouth tasted like sawdust, I couldn't make it go down my clenched throat. I coughed and spit it across the linen tablecloth.

"Jennifer stop that right now, take a drink of water why don't you. What is wrong with you? You look like you saw a ghost or something." Her voice rose in anger as her brown eyes demanded cooperation.

"But mama, please, I don't want to live with them."

My face was now contorted with the fear and anger that threatened to strike out at her. "Mama please can't we just stay here? Please mama, don't make me live there."

"What in the world is going on with you? I have no idea why you are sitting there like a dummy crying about something that should make you happy. You're acting like the world has just come to an end or something. I just don't understand you and I never will. Can't I ever have anything the way I want it in this life? What about my happiness, huh, what about me? Don't I count for anything at all? All I ever have to do is think about you kids. Well I'm sick of it. We're moving and that's the end of this discussion. Do you understand me Jennifer?" Mama was standing up, her hands braced against the table, her words beating into me. She grabbed her plate and took it over to the sink. She want to hear another word from you. Do you hear me? Just go upstairs and get in bed. Now move it." I screamed again and again throwing myself on the linoleum floor and pounding my fists angrily. "Get off that floor this instant and get yourself to bed. I don't know why you have to always make things so hard for me. Why can't I ever be happy. Now get up and get out of here!" She pulled me in the direction of the stairs. I screamed out my hatred for her all the way to my room where I lay in bed and eventually cried myself to sleep.

For days I moped around the house, refusing to eat or talk. Mama treated me as she always had, with distant caring. I thought and thought about what to do to make things different. I could not imagine the reality of living under his roof. I knew things would only get worse if I were so easily available to him. I considered telling someone about what he did to me but quickly dismissed it. I knew first of all that no one would believe me and secondly that they would blame me and hate me forever. He had me exactly where he wanted me, stuck in a secret terror that knew no release.

A week went by before mama mentioned moving again. Not looking at me she mumbled,"We are moving a week from this coming Saturday. I expect you to pack up your toys next week." I stared at her silently, wishing she were dead. "I know you are not thrilled about this move but we are doing it anyway. I have to save money or we won't be able to go to California in June. So this is what we must do and I expect you to be a good girl and behave for your grandparents. Do you hear me Jennifer?"

For many minutes I sat there in heavy silence, tears streaming down my face, my fingers digging savagely into my palms. "I'm not moving and you can't make me. If you try I'll run away and you'll never see me again." My words sounded dull and meaningless.

"I forbid you to argue with me any further Jennifer. You will bite your tongue and do as you are told. It's time you learned you can't always have things your way."

Shrieks of anger and hatred poured from my mouth. My words came out in torrents of passionate fury. "I hate you. I hate your guts. Grandpa touches me and you don't even care. You probably even told him to do it. I hate you and I hate him and I'm not ever moving." I looked up to find her staring at me as though I were some kind of crazed animal. I couldn't believe I had actually said those words out loud. It was as though a tidal wave had been unleashed and could not be controlled. "He kisses me and touches me and does all kinds of ugly stuff to me. You don't even care, I know you don't. You could make him stop but you never do. You leave me with him and then he does it more and more." Still she said nothing. Her mouth hung open, her eyes burned with surfacing violence. "Mama don't you hear me? Grandpa touches my private parts and makes me touch his. I hate it but he won't stop. He does it all the time. Whenever he has a chance. Oh mama please don't make me live with him." I'm so scared of him, he hurts me so badly." I sat on the couch, rocking frantically back and forth, my hands pulling at my hair. Still she sat across from me looking like a statue frozen in movement. I screamed at the top of my lungs, "Mama don't you hear me? Please mama make him stop. I hate it mama, it makes me feel so dirty and ugly. Please mama it's not my fault he just won't stop. I tell him to all the time but he won't listen to me. Mama, please! Mama! Mama, please!"

Mama stood up abruptly, her eyes red and ice cold. Her body shook and her hands clutched at her dress as she yelled at me shrilly. "Stop it! Stop telling me those horrible lies right this minute. You're really sick and I'm going to take you to a psychiatrist tomorrow. Don't you dare say another word, just get out of my sight this second. You're a liar and you know it. You're trying to kill me but I, won't let you, now get out of here."

I ran crying hysterically up the stairs to my room. Slamming the door behind me, I flung myself on the bed wailing uncontrollably. Mama never came near me the rest of the night. As I cried myself to sleep, rocking my body soothingly, I knew I had made yet another mistake by trusting mama with my terrible secret. Not only did she not believe me and thought me a crazy liar but now I felt she had totally rejected me.

The next morning mama and I avoided making any kind of contact with each other. As I sat picking at my breakfast across the table from her, neither of us spoke about what had happened the night before. Her eyes were as red as mine. She looked as though she had gotten as little sleep as I had. She gave me instructions for the day, routinely kissed my cheek and quickly left for work.

It was clear that we were to never again discuss the abusive relationship between Grandpa John and myself. We had an unspoken agreement; one that would end up hurting her almost as much as me. She was to deny my reality by labeling it a lie. I was to suffer at the hands of her father forever. A life sentence had been passed on us both.

A little more than a week later we moved into my grandparent's house. Mama and I shared the bedroom next to theirs. I was unsociable and sulky and cried without apparent cause. For days I would not utter a word, walking around with my shoulders hunched and my eyes cast to the ground. Other times I rambled non-stop. My aimless chatter became such a nuisance that grandpa offered to pay me a quarter for each half hour that I kept my mouth closed. I ate very little and lost more weight. I took several baths everyday and washed my hands repeatedly. I communicated through tears, temper tantrums and long periods of silence. The walls of my prison grew thicker and more isolating everyday. At night, lying next to mama in bed, I curled myself up into a tight fetal position and rocked myself to sleep. Mama and I laid there, each safely separate from the other, late into the evening hours. Mama with her protective dime store novel and me entrapped in my cocoon of secrets and silences.

The planning and preparation for the move was well under way. Mama and Grandma Sarah shopped and packed steadily. When they went out at night to attend a church function or for endless hours of shopping I was left in grandpa's care. So many evenings I begged mama to stay home with me or at least take me along with her. I clung desperately to her skirts as she walked out the door leaving me with supposedly reassuring words of her quick return. Often I persisted to the point of being dragged across the floor on the hem of her dress until she screamed at me to leave her alone and proceeded out the door.

I believed on one level that she knew that what I had told her was true. It felt as though she was sacrificing me to her father. At those moments I hated her even more violently than I did her father. I made hopeless vows of revenge as I plotted how best to hurt her like she was hurting me.

On those nights I was forced to be alone with. Grandpa John I tried to avoid being anywhere near him. I barricaded the door to my room, turned the radio on, and buried myself in a novel. Often I locked myself in the bathroom taking long scalding baths. Many evenings grandpa did not approach me and we passed the evening never seeing each other. It was the other times that caused scarring memories.

Feb 17, 1962

Dear Diary,

I hate living here. I wish I were dead.

March 26, 1962

Dear Diary,

Mama had to go to school for a conference with my teacher and she's really mad at me. She says that I had better straighten up or else. Big deal, what can she do to me that she hasn't already done. I hate her more all the time. I don't know what the big deal is, I'm still making all A's on my report card. So what if I don't talk to anyone. I don't have anything to say that anyone wants to hear, so why bother talking.

March 31, 1962

Dear Diary,

Mama took me to see old Dr. Gilpin because I have lost too much weight, and because I keep complaining about being sick. He said it's just a part of growing up and that there's nothing to worry about. Debbie called last night. She broke her leg at school. Mama got all upset and said she should be out there with her kids. What about me, she never seems to care about me when I'm sick. Mama said she loved me last night. I just cried. I don't believe her and never will. Grandma Sarah is going to give my hair a hot oil treatment tonight. She says

*she never saw such dull hair on a little girl before. Sometimes
I think she's trying to be nice to me. She probably thinks I am
crazy too. Mama sure does.*

I am sitting on the bed I share with mama reading <u>A Tree
Grows in Brooklyn</u> for the third time this month. I hear heavy
footsteps coming up the stairs. The door suddenly is thrust open.
Grandpa John is standing here looking at me. "Come down
stairs and watch television with me Jen." It is more an order than
a request.

"No grandpa. I really need to finish this book for school tomorrow." I am shaking inside, praying he won't see the title and
know I'm lying.

"I didn't ask you girl, I'm telling you. So get down there!" I
know better than to argue with him. I follow him slowly down
the wooden stairway into the living room. The TV is on, tuned
into Red Skelton. I take my place on the carpeted floor a few feet
from the set. Grandpa is standing here next to me, sweat is beginning to form on my brow. All I see are white shoes, white belt.
Brown baggy pants hanging loosely from his hips. Off-white un-
dershirt complete with grease spots over a slightly bulging stomach. He is mouthing something I can't quite make out.

"I'm talking to you Jen, so you better listen. You don't need to
make me mad tonight, do you? Now stand up and dance for me
like I said." He is removing his belt, it hangs in his hand threat-
eningly. A lit cigarette dangles from the corner of his mouth as he
grabs my hand pulling me to my feet. He crosses the room and
sits on the couch watching me carefully. I stand here, my feet
rooted in the carpet. "Dance Jennifer! Don't make me madder
than I am." His words hold a threat I know he means. Still I stand
here motionless. He is getting up, crossing the room, each step of
his white shoes digging into the carpet brings him closer and
closer. All I can see are his white shoes with brown. soles getting

nearer and nearer. But all too soon white and red are flashing brilliantly before my eyes. "Dance Jenny!." His voice is coming from somewhere inside the whiteness. It is loud and demanding, hues of fiery red dance from his tongue. "God damn it I told you to dance."

A small, frightened girl stands here. Her stance defiantly immobilized, her hands on hips, her chin jutted out, her face hidden behind tangled dark hair. "No! Leave me alone!" the girl is protesting. Is that person me? She is clawing at her face, nails tearing at the corners of her eyes. I know she is me; the pain of her self-assault shatters my separation. The white belt is whipped out, lashing at my arms. An angry welt swells.

"God dammit dance or I'll beat the crap out of you." I move ever so slowly, arms rising to my side, knees bending and swaying gently. My face distorted beyond recognition; tears run down to wet my straggled hair. "Take your clothes off stupid! You know what I mean, now do it!" His roar echoes in my ears, red vibrations crashing around me. I move slowly, as if in a trance, undoing one button at a time. Slowly, too slowly for his needs. The white belt wildly aimed, lands on my cheek. I hurry now, fingers tripping over each other until the pajama top is freed from my bony shoulders. My feet quicken at the sight of the whiteness before me. He steps on my bare toes, white trails left there to ferment and rot. I am lost in a world of swirling reds and whites. "The pants you fool, take of your pants!" I bend slightly at the waist, not fast enough for him and the white belt forms another welt on my bare back.

"No! I'm not going to! I don't want to and you can't make me!" I am screaming thunderously as I run towards the stairs. He is chasing me, dragging me, kicking and yelling back into the living room. I stare at him rebelliously. My heart is pounding fiercely. My head feels too heavy for my neck.

"I don't want to have to hurt you Jenny. All I want is for you to undress and dance a little bit. Is that too much to ask. I love you and I want to see your pretty body. Now come on, move it for grandpa."

"But grandpa, I hate it. I don't want you to touch me, please grandpa, please just let me go upstairs."

"I'm not going to touch you, I just want you to dance. Can't you do that for me after all I've done for you? If you dance I promise not to lay a hand on you, okay?"

He is bargaining with me and I know it. If I let him watch me dance naked then I won't have to endure his hands or mouth on me. My pajama bottoms dangle loosely around my knees. I step out of them in time to avoid more flashes of red and white. His hand is moving up and down over the weapon he has pulled from his underwear. He stands not even two feet away. All I can hear is the liquid like rasp of his breathing. It reminds me of the time I visited the ocean. I try to pretend I am once again standing on the soft sand. I force the sand between my toes, losing myself in the crash of the surf beating against the shore.

"Don't stop God dammit! His hand is a blur of movement, going faster and faster. I run for the stairs, screeching loud animal sounds. His arms, rough and hairy, grab me around the belly, and throw me to the floor. "Jenny, oh Jenny, why do you make me do this? All I want is to love you, can't you see that? Damn it, cooperate and everything will be fine. You can make this horrible or wonderful. It's all up to you. Now just dance will you please!" His hand is again rubbing, jumping frantically over himself.

I am dancing, slowly gyrating, undulating to the music of his hand action. Finally the music ends abruptly with a surge of sticky white fluid that lands on my stomach. Shrieks, red, burning gasps of degradation gush from the soul of the dirtied little girl.

"Go on Jenny, get out of here!"

I run up the stairs to my room, cowering under the blankets on my bed. It is dark and cold here. I feel nasty and ashamed. Time passes slowly. I don't know how long I have been lying here before I hear his steps on the stairs.

"Jenny" he whispers into the darkened room. I slide further under the covers, holding my shaking body. As he reaches out to touch my back my body spasms in fear. What more does he want from me? He promised to leave me alone now. "Come here honey, I want to hold you." His voice is deceptively warm and convincing.

I yell back, "Go away. I hate you! Leave me alone!"

"I'm sorry I made you do that, I promise not to do it again. Come up here please, let me hold you. I love you so much honey. You're so special to me. But sometimes I can't control myself around you. You're so beautiful and I need you so much." His voice is hypnotic as he begs me to be close to him. I battle with my need to be comforted and the knowledge that he could give me nothing but more pain. I want to punish him for making me feel so dirty.

"Get away from me! I hate your stinking guts!" I hurl at him as he silently walks out the door.

Mama came home to find me still buried under the covers crying. When she asked what was wrong I didn't answer. I wanted to make her worry about me, I wanted her to suffer. I hated her and everyone else.

Most of the time when grandpa approached me I was in my bedroom. It didn't matter whether the light was out and I was pretending to be or actually was asleep. His molestations began in the same manner. He would sit on the edge of the bed, pull the blankets away from my body and slip his hand underneath my layers of pajamas. Some of these times were easier, more endurable than others. These nights he would fondle me while he touched himself, saying barely a word in response to my pleas for him to stop. When he was done he would leave as silently as he had entered. These were by far the least painful of his night time visits and for the most part I was able to escape into the ceiling above me.

The other scenes are agony from the start. Grandpa has his rough hands all over me; rubbing, probing, man-handling me everywhere. He is pulls his pants down to his knees. He never removes them completely. I am pushing him away with powerless arms. He of course is winning and undressing me. I am lying here naked and ashamed, searching for a sanctuary above me. He is muttering under his breath those words reserved only for these occasions. He is kissing my lips, forcing his tongue between my teeth then working down to my neck, chest and genitals with his wet, slimy lips. He seems to like kissing my private parts best of all. His breathing is growing loud and heavy. I feel a spreading warmth down below. I quickly make myself separate from the possible pleasure. My self-hatred and disgust will not allow my body to feel anything but the knot of anger in the pit of my stomach. He is lying on top of me, bruising me with his weight, sucking on my newly forming breasts and handling himself. He is inching his way down again, stopping to bury his face between my legs. I am watching safely from my spot above the bed. He moves again, trying to force the ugliness of his body into my mouth. He shudders suddenly and gluey liquid pours on my face. He is getting up, fastening his pants in place. He is tiptoeing out the door. Turning to look at me, he whispers loud enough to be heard, how sorry he is.

I would lie there sobbing for hours. His need to be forgiven meant nothing to me. None of it mattered anymore. I was his personal plaything. He toyed with me and used me as he desired. I would then get up and take yet another steaming bath to cleanse myself of his touch. I was completely powerless and vulnerable to Grandpa John. No matter how violently I protested his assaults, my resistance was in vain because he was so much bigger and stronger than I. He always got exactly what he wanted.

Week after week, month after month, it was the same. He molested me. I resisted. I cried, screamed and fought. I eventually gave in to his control. I took baths that burned my skin. Nothing I said or did made any difference. He owned me. I was his to do with as he pleased. No one was going to rescue me We both accepted this reality. Gradually I gave into my fate. I grew passive and dull. I succeeded in deadening my mind and body. Or so I thought.

April 5, 1962

Dear Diary,

Yesterday I rode the bus uptown. I walked all around Times Square and rode the elevator to the top of the Empire State building. Afterwards I went shopping and bought five books and a new diary for the trip to California. I'm going to save the rest of my money to buy souvenirs while we are on vacation. I am starting to feel excited about moving. At least there mama and I will not have to live with grandma or anyone else except Debbie and David. I hope Jimmy is able to spend time with us. I miss him. I don't have any friends anymore. I don't know why but nobody seems to like me. I don't really care but once in awhile I feel lonely. I don't have anything in common with the kids in my class any-

way but still I would like someone to be my friend. At least once in awhile.

April 28, 1962

Dear Diary,

The principal sent a note home from school saying that I had come out second in the testing we had to do last month. He said that he is recommending I skip a grade and go straight into the sixth grade next year. Mama said she was proud of how smart I am but she does not believe in children skipping grades. She says its not good for them. I like the idea of skipping. It would mean I could get out of school a year earlier and that would be great. I have decided for sure that I will be an actress when I grow up. When we get to California I am going to take acting classes.

I was not quite ten years old the first time my grandfather raped me. I never imagined that his attacks could be worse than they already were. How very young and naive I was. It began like all the other times.

I am sitting on my bed, doing homework. Mama and Grandma Sarah are out shopping. I hear the door open, and turn my head to see Grandpa John entering the room. My first reaction is panic, "Oh God, what does he want now." My stomach is twisting painfully and my throat tightens to cut off the air. As he places himself on the edge of the mattress I strain to catch my breath. I can not look at him. I continue to focus unseeingly on the open geography book before me. He is reaching out, his hands stroking my hair. I move, as if struck by lightning, to the opposite side of the bed.

"What are you reading?" he asks quietly.

"I'm doing homework. I have to have it done by tomorrow or I'll get in a lot of trouble. I'm already behind." I stammer quickly. I cling to the hope that he would hear my pleas and leave.

"Do you know how much I still love you little girl? I do, you know, even though things haven't been so good between us lately, I still love you more than anyone else."

His voice is soft. It has that trance-like tone I have learned to fear. I say nothing, still staring at the pages lying open on the bed. I am trying to will myself far away from him. He is lowering his hand to cup my chin, forcing my eyes to meet his. I glare back with eyes brimming with hatred.

"Get out of here and leave me alone!", I blurt out, my voice capturing all the anger and fear I feel.

"What's wrong Jenny? You used to be so happy to see me. You used to beg for me to hold you. Now you act like you don't even like me anymore. How come you treat your grandpa so badly lately?"

"It doesn't matter, just leave me alone."

"But I love you Jen, you know that. This is my way of showing you just how much I care about you." His voice flows over me like maple syrup. I am fighting with myself to stay angry. Part of me wants to give in and get it over with quickly. If only for a brief moment I too need to feel loved and wanted. Still I despise him and what he does to me.

"Just go away! You know I can't stand to look at you!"

His eyes are brimming with tears, the blueness spilling on to his cheeks.

"Oh Jen, it makes me feel so bad that you act so mean to

me. You're the only thing that I have. I need you."

"I said get out of here, if you don't, I'm going to tell mama." I threaten him weakly, knowing very well the emptiness of my warning.

"You won't tell her, we both know that. Even if you did, she wouldn't believe you over me. Besides there's nothing wrong with my loving you. You know I love you more than she does. That's all that matters, isn't it? If your mama loved you wouldn't she be home with you now? No, it's me that spends so much time with you. Not your precious mother." He is bargaining with me. "I'll do anything you want you know."

"If you'll do anything for me then just leave me alone. I don't want you to do that stuff anymore, I hate it."

"You don't have to do anything Jenny just let me make you feel good. You know I only want you to be happy. Just take your clothes off and let me love you, okay? I want to teach you something new tonight."

I don't budge. My arms are firmly locked around my chest. My knees are bent to protect me like a shield. He is reaching out to unbutton my pajama top. "Stop it! I told you no! I don't want to do that crap anymore. I have a lot of homework to do so just leave your creepy hands off me!"

"Jen I don't want to have to force you but I will If you don't do as you're told. I know you want me as much as I want you. Your little act doesn't fool me a bit. You want to please grandpa don't you?"

"Please grandpa not tonight. I just can't take anymore. You're making me crazy! Besides I don't feel well. I feel kind of sick and stuff. Please just let me study and go to sleep. If you loved me as much as you say you do then you'd let me be. Please grandpa. please."

Apparently Grandpa John is not willing to bargain or try to cajole me any further. His hands are grasping me, tearing open the front of my pajama top while I vainly try to push him away. He has overpowered me once again. I lie here on the bed, naked, curled into a rigid ball fighting back the tears with the palms of my hands. I am trying to find my spot on the ceiling, trying to disappear into my fantasy haven. The sound of his zipper and heavy breathing forces my heart to pound wildly. He jerks my head around to face him. The terror I feel doubles immediately. Something is very different tonight. He has completely removed his pants. His stiffened penis wavers in front of my mouth. I shut my eyes and scream savagely. He is positioning himself on the bed next to me, pushing me onto my back, using his hands to pry open my legs.

"Come on Jen, this isn't going to hurt. It will feel real good honey. Just lie still and let me show you how wonderful love can be."

"I hate you." my words are as empty as the child who lays in dread of his attack.

"Oh honey, stop that bullshit, I know you love me. I want to show you something new tonight, something you're really going to like." He's whispering in my ear, burrowing his face in my hair. He is rolling over on top of me, pinning me under his massive weight. I am unable to keep my sobbing under control. I yell out at the top of my lungs. He is paying no attention to me. He kisses my neck and mouth roughly, running his tongue around in circles down my chest. He lingers at my breasts before reaching my private parts.

"Please grandpa, please don't please!" He seems not to hear me. I want to run but I have learned there is no escape from his torture. I am praying for mama to come home and save me. I try to find my wonderful Cleaver-like family but they are as lost to me as mama is. I am lying corpse-like, begging that he get whatever it is he wants over with quickly and as painlessly as possible.

Grandpa's face is close to mine now. His breath is hot and foul in my face. He is red and puffy. He grabs his penis and shoves it between my clenched legs. His whole body is grinding into mine. He is too heavy, he is too big.

"Stop it, please stop it! You're killing me! Still he doesn't hear me, doesn't stop. He is forcing my legs apart even wider. I know they are about to break. I cry out in pain, tears pour on to my twisted face. "Please grandpa, stop it! You're hurting me!" I feel him try to enter me. I try to close my legs against his hammering assault. I scream out in primitive anguish as he pierces my vaginal walls.

"Oh God! Please! No! No! Help me, God, please! Grandpa please, it hurts. You're killing me. Stop! No No!" My screams go unnoticed as he lunges at me over and over again. I feel as though my whole body is being ripped apart. I am faint and on the verge of vomiting. I pound my fists against his back, scraping flesh off with my nails. He remains oblivious to my pain. He doesn't even look at me. I bite into his fleshy arms viciously and beat my fists into his back.

He is crying out and falling limply against me. His dead weight is nearly smothering me but at least the wrenching pain has lessened. I scream, bite and wail my fists trying to free my body from his suffocating trap.

Minutes have passed. He is rolling off me. I lay here bruised and battered against the stained sheets. My hating eyes curse him silently as I crawl off the bed, curl myself up into a ball crouched in the corner of the room. I am holding myself tightly, knees to chest and rocking slowly back and forth. My face is buried in my knees soaking them with tears, I don't look at him but I hear the sounds of his dressing. As he quietly shuts the door behind him I hear him whisper very softly, "I'm so sorry Jenny."

May 29, 1962

Dear Diary,

Today is my tenth birthday. I am a whole decade old but it doesn't really feel any different. I wonder how come people always ask, "How does it feel to be ten years old?" What a dumb question. It feels just like nine does. Mama took me out for dinner tonight. I got to choose anything I wanted so naturally I had chinese food. Mama gave me some summer clothes and a few books as gifts. I can't wait to move to California. As far as I'm concerned the sooner the better. I am never coming back to New York as long as I live. I hate this city. Everything here is ugly and dirty.

June 13, 1962

Dear Diary,

We are on our way to sunny California. Hurray! This morning before we left, a group of friends from church and the neighborhood came to see us off. Everyone was crying and wishing us well in our new home. I am so excited I can hardly sit still. Mama and grandma have decided that we will make this trip a real vacation and stop off and see all the tourist attractions along the way. I can't wait to see the Grand Canyon. I've heard it's beautiful. We are also going to Mount Rushmore, Dodge City and the Petrified Forest. I think that everything is going to be alright from now on. As long as I never have to come back to Columbus Avenue, life will be perfect. When we turned the corner today, I made myself not look back at the ugly street. It's weird though, it kind of feels like I'm leaving part of me back there sitting on the fire escape. I hope its's the bad part. God I hated living there. I hate that whole city. Mama and grandma are both in really good moods.

They are laughing and everything. I haven't heard mama laugh in a long time. I have the whole back seat to myself so I can spread out and write in this diary. I am looking out the window watching the countryside roll by, I've never seen anything so beautiful. The farther we get from New York the happier I feel. I just know that things are going to be better now. California is the land of dreams that come true. That's what grandma says anyway and I think she might be right. Once we are living there, by ourselves, everything will be fine. I can't wait!

Our destination for the first day on the road was Youngstown, Pennsylvania. Grandpa John sat behind the wheel of his big yellow Chevrolet whistling the miles away. The four of us seemed to be quite excited and shared a playfully good mood. I tentatively ventured out of my isolation as I felt unusually safe surrounded by mama and Grandma Sarah. I was confident that grandpa would not make any demands on me while we travelled since we would all be together throughout the trip.

After our arrival in Youngstown we went to Howard Johnsons for clam dinners before returning to our hotel for the evening. Since I had never spent the night in a hotel before I was totally thrilled and keyed up. My only concern was that grandpa would be sleeping in the same room with mama and me. Still I believed I was not in any real danger since I would be sharing a bed with mama. I bathed and changed into two pairs of pajamas before turning on the TV As I settled in I noticed mama changing her clothes. My throat closed tightly around the words that forced their way out.

"Mama why are you changing? Aren't you coming to bed now? Huh mama?"

"No honey, grandma and I are going out to do a little shopping." Her intentions were a direct assault on my frail sense of security. My shattered confidence gave way to engulfing fear.

"Oh mama please don't go." Tears were building behind already reddened eyes as I begged her, once again, not to leave me alone with her father. "Please stay here with me mama. Please mama can't you just stay here with me and watch TV Okay mama?"

"We won't be gone long honey, don't worry. I'll bring you something real special for a souvenir," was her monotone response to my pleas for her presence. It was true that every time she went shopping she bought nice presents, but I didn't want her gifts. I wanted her, I needed her. Nothing else but her being in the same room could keep me safe from him.

"Then can I go with, you? Please mama, can I go too? I really want to and I'll be real good I promise, okay mama, okay?" I begged in my most whining voice.

"No. You just stay here and keep grandpa company. We'll be back in just a little while."

"No, I don't want to. Please," I cried "please let me go with you. Please!"

"I told you no Jennifer. How many times do I have to tell you. You know grandpa gets lonely when we go out. Now you be a good girl and take care of grandpa while we're gone. We won't be gone long and I'll bring you a nice surprise," she stated emphatically.

"No! I don't want to stay here with him and I don't want your stupid presents either! Please just let me go with you. Please just this once! I sulked and pounded my fists on the bed.

"Jennifer you just calm yourself down right now! Quit working yourself up into a tizzy for nothing."

For the fifteen minutes it took them to finish getting ready to leave me with him I continued to beg and plead to go along. I

even resorted to a full-blown temper tantrum which only succeeded in making her even angrier and more anxious to go without me. She did not relent. She quickly planted a kiss on my
sullen face and left me alone with her father. I followed her out
the door and into the parking lot and was left standing there,
with the cool summer wind blowing through my pajamas, staring at the car's tail lights fading into the distance. I sat on the
curb, watching the passing traffic and wishing I were with someone, anyone else. If it hadn't been for the skimpiness of my clothing and the coolness of the evening I would have sat out there
until my mother's return but the elements forced me to return to
the motel room.

I snuck quietly, stealthily, into the room to find grandpa sitting
in a chair watching the Red Skelton Show. I hurried into bed,
yanking the blankets up to my chin. I sat there silently, pretending to watch the show while actually keeping one eye alerted to
grandpa. I was painfully aware of trying not to make the slightest noise. Gathering all my willpower I tried to make myself disappear but my fear of grandpa's oppressive silence prevented
the flight. For awhile, I thought maybe I had really made myself
invisible. He didn't seem to know I was in the room. During a
commercial he turned to face me but didn't say a word. I held my
body rigidly as he stared in my direction. When he focused his
attention back to the television set I felt the tension ease slightly.
My fingers had been so clenched that my nails left angry red
marks on the palms of my hands. Redness slowly left my skin as
I relaxed the grip I held on myself.

Watching, always aware of him. What is he going to do to me?
What does he want? Will he be gentle or will he hurt me again?
He seems totally intent on watching the TV show but is he re-
ally? Please grandpa, please don't hurt me anymore.

The TV show is over. He is getting up, switching the set off
with one hand, and turning to face me. Panic. Oh God, no!
Please, no! Grabbing myself tightly, hold on Jenny. Close yourself off. Go now, run! Stomach rumbling, knots in my bowel.
Heart beating wildly, thump, thump, thump against my temples.

"Take your clothes off! Anger shooting from his ovaled mouth. "Don't look at me that way, God damn it, just do what I say!"

I force myself to ignore him, trying to erase the hatred from my face, watching the rising of my chest against the blanket.

"God dammit I told you to take off your clothes! Take them off or I'll take them off for you!"

"No." My anger as vehement as his now. "You can't make me either! Just leave me the hell alone."

"You little brat! How dare you talk back to me when I'm the only one who loves you. You just do as I say or you'll be sorrier than you've ever been."

"I'm not ever going to do what you tell me again. I hate you. You make me sick!"

"I'm warning you Jenny, you do as I tell you to or I'll teach you a lesson about who's in charge around here! Do you understand me young lady?"

"I don't care what you say or what you do! You've already ruined my life anyway. What difference does any of it make?"

"Stop bellyaching Jenny, Just take your pajamas off and let me see your beautiful body." His tone is now softer, his blue eyes moist and pleading.

"Jenny I love you so much. I don't mean to get so mad at you but you make me do it. If you would let me I would be real nice to you. How about it honey?"

"Leave me alone! I hate you!"

As I spit my disgust in his face I watched a sheepish grin form suddenly and then just as quickly saw him try to cover it, as though it had never really been there. That was his way, his motto so to speak, always pretend to be what you are not. He turned abruptly, walking out the door and slamming it behind him. A warm, liquidy rush of victory spread over me. I had won, he was obviously as afraid of me as I was of him. If only I had known it would be so easy to prevent his attack with my words I would have done so before. Still something didn't fit. As heady with triumph as I felt my body refused to relax. Heated tension, grinding confusion keeping me bent over as I lay in a ball-like position.

Head facing away, the click of the door opening echoes throughout the small enclosure. Turning, jumping up, running too late. Rope around my stomach, my arms, biting into my flesh. Screaming,"No, no please no." Long painful sounds escape from deep inside me. "Grandpa, grandpa, please don't! Oh God, please." Tears blinding my way, clawing my way off the floor where he has flung me.

Biting him, feeling his white hairy flesh between my grinding teeth. "Let go you little bitch!" Biting, gnawing through his skin. Head being yanked back, hair almost pulled out. Screams, curses flying across the room. His breathing is hard and irregular as he lifts me up and carries me to the bed. Ropes burning holes in my arms. More rope cutting into my ankles as he ties them together.

"Let me go you son of a bitch. I hate you!" Using the language he has used on me, shrieking my loathing, hurling waves of hatred in his face. "You prick! I hate your rotten guts! Leave me alone! Let me go!"

"You'll see never to talk like that again. Couldn't let me love you like I wanted to, huh, well you'll see now you little bitch." His words are quick, his face bright red. More rope capturing me around the neck, knotting my wrists together. Pulling at his balding white head, digging my nails into his skull. His scarf of blue and white is pulled tightly around my mouth. Yelling into the scarf the muffled grunts of my anguish. Helpless. Can't move my arms or legs, hands tied together. Images of baby calves at the rodeo appear before me. Tossing, turning, kicking into the bed, aiming at grandpa as he unzips his pants and pulls out his weaponry.

He rolls me onto my side, "Just stay there you little slut, just lay there and watch. "This could be your asshole. But now you don't get it, just watch and wish, if you be good now I'll let you have it next time." Closing my eyes, desperately trying to get away from him. Please mama come home, please some one make him stop, it hurts, please mama. "I told you to watch me! open up those God damn eyes before I beat the crap out of you! Eyes shut, no, no. A stinging slap across my face. Eyes forced open to see his hand flailing over himself. His face is a contorted mask of grimacing ugliness, wet beads dangling from his nose. "I'm in charge here little girl and don't you forget it. You better learn to do what I tell you to. You are such a bad little girl, I don't know how come I love you. You aren't worth it you know."

No words, just breathing, heaving, wheezing labored breaths. Close my eyes and pretend, oh God, try to imagine I am far away from here. Good, can't hear anymore. The silence is deafening. Remember how beautiful the mountains were when we drove through them today, how brightly the sun shone on their purple slopes. Such a nice day, everyone happy and carefree. Moans, low, pained moaning. I even saw some cows grazing off in the distance, some horses too. I'd really like to ride a horse. Grunts, guttural sobs. When I grow up I'm going to buy a horse and ride it everyday. I'm going to live in a house where I can have lots of horses and other animals too. Hot, sticky, oozing liquid dripping off my eyebrows onto my eyes. Feet crossing the room, water running. Feet recrossing, untying of ropes, feet freed, scarf loosened. Sticky liquid gluing my eyes together. Scarf wiping it away, body immobilized in a far away place of horses and freedom.

"Get up and clean yourself off!" No movement from the shell on the bed. "Go on girl. Get up!"

I move slightly, crossing the room, following his tracks to the bathroom, locking the door behind me, filling the tub with scorching water.

"Jennifer! Jennifer! Are you alright?" Mother's voice, mother's fists pounding on the door? "Jennifer answer me! Jennifer!" More beating against the wood. "Jennifer you answer me right now, do you hear me, Jennifer!"

"What?" Someone with a ghost-like voice came from deep inside of me to respond to her.

"Jennifer come out of there right now. Do you hear me? Come on out of there!" I buried myself in the now tepid water imagining I was Lloyd Bridges on Sea Hunt.

"Jennifer come out right now! What is wrong with you? Are you deaf or something?" Her voice bounces off the walls of the bathtub sounding so funny that I laugh and choke on the water that rushes into my mouth. "Jennifer, please, Jennifer come out of there. Please honey, I want you to see the lovely dress I bought for you."

Our 'vacation' lasted another week. Though I know that we stopped at all the tourist attractions I don't remember much of it at all. I do recall that the next time mother and grandma went out to shop I locked myself in the hotel bathroom until they got back. The only other thing that really stands out for me is that once, while unloading suitcases from the trunk, I saw the ropes lying unobtrusively on the bottom. It was then, while standing there rubbing back tears with my fists that I decided never to cry again. I wasn't about to give him the satisfaction of seeing me suffer.

July 7, 1962

Dear Diary,

It is so different here, I'm not sure I really like it. Sure the sun shines almost everyday and the beaches are really beautiful but strangely enough I miss rowhouses and fire escapes. We have been staying in the country with Aunt Lorraine, Sonny and Uncle Danny since we arrived last week. Sonny is much sicker than he was when I last saw him. They are even talking about having to get him a walker so that he can get around by himself. It's really sad to see him so unhappy I don't think I want to change places with him anymore. Tomorrow Aunt Lorraine is taking Debbie, Sonny and I to the beach for a picnic.

Aug. 2, 1962

Dear Diary,

Mama got a job in a photography studio in Long Beach so we are moving there next weekend. She rented one half of a duplex so that Aunt Lorraine, Uncle Danny, Sonny and her parents can move in next door. I don't know why mama is so afraid to live without them. I hate it. I really want to live off by ourselves. Jimmy has been coming over on weekends and bringing a couple of his Army buddies with him. Jimmy looks so different now. I guess he's grown up. He told mama last night that he will probably be going overseas to Japan in a few months. Mama cried. Mama got a letter from Peter, who says he wants to come out here and be with her. If she says yes, I'll just die.

About a month after we settled into our new home in Long Beach the rest of our relatives moved in next door. I spent most of the summer playing with Sonny or lounging in the back yard reading books. There didn't seem to be many places to go so everyone was home much more than in New York. Mama would not allow me to roam the city on the bus as she had back home so I was pretty much stuck. Debbie and David seemed to be having as difficult a time making friends as I was and though they didn't welcome my presence they were forced to tolerate me. Mama worked during the day so Grandma Sarah and Aunt Lorraine were left in charge of me. I saw grandpa only when I had to which usually meant family dinners or while I was outside playing. Sometimes I would watch him watching me through the large front window of his house. He sat and stared mutely, while I either pretended not to notice him or glared back with hateful eyes.

I was careful never to be alone with Grandpa John. When he did babysit it was for both Sonny and I and he never approached me during those times. When he made Sonny go to bed before me I avoided him by falling back on the trick I had learned on our trip; I locked myself in the bathroom with a book until mama's return. I began to feel as though I had some control over the situation.

Sept. 10, 1962

Dear Diary,

I started the fifth grade today, it was so boring. I've never seen a school like this one, it looks more like a summer camp than the big brick buildings I am used to. From my desk I can see litter free streets lined with palm trees and rolling green hills off in the distance. In some ways I wish there were trash cans lying in dirty gutters and steel skyscrapers instead. It's strange but I sort of miss New York, not Columbus Avenue though. I'm still never going back to that street ever again. The kids in my class are weird too, they act like spoiled little rich brats. They kept making fun of my accent and clothes.

I don't care though because I don't like them either. Who needs them. My teacher is real creepy too. He's at least seventy years old and wears big flowered ties that make him look more like a clown than a teacher. I wish I had a woman teacher. I hate men, they are all nasty. I was so bored today. We learned all the stuff Mr. Barker talked about in school last year. Oh well, at least it will be easy. Jimmy is leaving for Japan next week. I am going to miss him. He's the only one who can make me laugh.

Nov. 18, 1962

Dear Diary,

I ditched school for the first time today It was great fun. I was on my way to walk to school when I found Debbie and David hiding behind the garage. It was a riot! They were both totally surprised that I caught them and bribed me into not telling mama by letting me stay home too. We sat around all day and watched TV and ate goodies. It sure was better than boring old Mr. Barker. I asked Mama if I could have a bike for Christmas but I doubt if she will because they are too expensive. Remember what I used to think happened to me. The really nasty stuff, well I think maybe I was just imagining it or maybe dreaming because so far nothing has happened here. Maybe there is a God after all.

———————————————

Christmas time was near and still grandpa hadn't been able to get me alone. He did seem to be watching me more closely than ever. While eating dinner with the whole family I could sense his eyes boring into me and the shakiness inside me would start all over again. Looking up, I saw him staring at my growing breasts and a cold wave of nausea swept through me. Whenever this happened I was immediately sickened by the food before me and was unable to swallow anymore. I made sure not to look at him again but still I felt him seeing right through me. When he looked at me like that I felt dirty and ashamed.

Although I was still quite withdrawn I was no longer feeling the terror of his constant assaults. As more and more time passed without being molested I grew increasingly confident that it would never happen again. Often I pretended that it had never really happened at all. Lying in bed at night I still took comfort in the world of my fantasies but the need for that escape was not quite so strong. I shared a room with Debbie and lying in bed next to her at night provided me with a small amount of security. I believed that grandpa couldn't get me if I was with her.

I finally got the bike I had long wanted that Christmas. It was old and ugly but it was a bike none the less. Mama couldn't afford to buy a new one so she had purchased a used one she found in the newspaper. David cleaned and painted it. Mama bought a horn and new tires so it looked as good as possible. While lying in bed Christmas Eve I heard a loud explosive sound coming from the living room. Mama quickly called out for me to stay put while Debbie joined her and David in the living room. A few seconds later I heard uproarious laughter coming from the three. I awoke the next morning to find my dream bike with one blown tire. David had filled it too full of air causing the explosion I had heard the night before. It was a good laugh for them but I was very disappointed since mama was unable to replace the tire for another month. Well at least I had a bike.

Sonny grew more helpless all the time. While we played army or cowboys and Indians he sat practically immobilized while I acted out all the parts for the both of us. He now used a walker to get around and had only partial use of his hands but little mobility anywhere else. It was terribly sad to watch him fade away like that. I pretended he was my baby brother and tried my best to take good care of him.

I felt the prison walls of my involvement with Grandpa John slowly crumble. For the first time in many years I was free to be a child again. Though I was not as open and carefree as before my sixth year, I felt safer than I had in a long, long time. I was finally away from Grandpa John, and I grew to like living in California. I was safe from his painful demands. I still needed and wanted mama more than she was able to give, but with no attacks by grandpa I was able to manage fairly well. I still kept a constant watch for him. I felt stifled around him and other men. I made sure I never had to be alone with any man except for Sonny. I knew they would only want the same things that Grandpa John did if given the chance. Sonny was the only safe male in my life.

School became easier as time passed. The novelty of my east coast accent wore off and I made friends with a few girls in my class. We attended a new Baptist church. Although I was no longer willing to attend regularly, I had figured out that what the preacher said in church and what the world was really like were two very different things. I was unable to accept the hypocrisy I saw. The contrasts were just too striking.

May 28, 1963

Dear Diary,

Tomorrow I will be eleven years old. Mama said we have to have a party with the whole family which I don't want to do. If I could do anything I wanted I would go out to dinner with mama and go to the movies afterwards. But mama always gets what she wants. Jimmy sent me a post card from Japan for my birthday. It's just wonderful. He won't be coming home for another six months, I wish it were sooner. David is graduating from high school this year and going to work right away. Mama says he should go to college but David said he's tired of school and just wants to make some money. When I graduate I'm going to college for sure. I want to be a teacher and work in France and travel all over the world. I'd like to own a ship and sail it everywhere. The only person who can come with me is Sonny. Mama says he won't live to be a grown up but I think she's wrong.

June 20, 1963

Dear Diary,

We have been in California a year now. I like it here more and more all the time. Mama found a better job and we moved here to Los Angeles. Our apartment is really neat. Next month the rest of the family is moving to L.A. too. Debbie's working for the summer and mama agreed that I am old enough to stay alone during the day while everyone is gone. I like being on my own with no one to tell me what to do. I am going to start babysitting for a little girl across the street. It will be nice to have money to spend again.

While at home alone I made sure to keep the door securely locked. I was afraid of unwanted visitors and especially for Grandpa John. My worst fear was that he would come over while I was home alone. The several times he actually did show up at our door I refused to let him in. I thought for sure he would tell mama and I would get in trouble for being rude to him but it was never mentioned.

I am lying here on my bed, the radio playing softly on the night table. I hear the front door opening slowly. Its creaking is scratchy and eerie. I race out to the living room. Grandpa John is there standing in front of the open door with a foolish grin plastered on his face.

"What are you doing here? How did you get in?"

"The door was open so I came in."

"No it wasn't. I just locked it a few minutes ago. Anyway I don't want you here so get out right now." My fear is quickly showing itself as anger.

"Now Jenny, we haven't been together in such a long time. Too long. I miss you so much. I just want to hold you on my lap like we used to. Okay? You know what I mean baby. I know how much you liked what we did." His voice is hauntingly familiar, sending rushes of cold down my back.

"No, go away! I don't want to sit with you. I don't even want to be in the same room with you. I hate you. Haven't you figured that out yet? Now just get the hell out of here or I'll call my mother."

"We both know what good that will do, don't we? Why the big show Jenny? I just want to be close to you. This past year without you has been awful. You remember how good it feels to love me. Don't you know that I'm still the only one who loves you." He is talking softly now as his footsteps come closer.

"I love you little girl, you'll always be mine Jennifer. No matter what, I'll always have you."

"Please grandpa just go away. We can't do that stuff anymore. It's not right and I don't like it." I am begging again as I slowly back up. I am afraid to run, afraid to stay put. I am immobilized. Old feelings of helplessness overtake me.

"Jenny, nothing has changed. Don't you see that? You still belong to me, that will never be any different. You know how special you are to me Jen. You know how much I love you." His voice continues to ooze out around me as he approaches where I am. Reaching out, his hand catches my shoulder. I find my strength and resist his power. With both arms he has captured me in his forceful embrace. I fight him with all the energy I can find, trying in vain to push him away.

"Jenny, Jenny honey it's okay. It's just grandpa. There's nothing to be afraid of. I love you, don't fight with me. Don't I make you feel good. Just relax and let me show you how wonderful loving can be." He is holding me tightly against his chest while whispering in my ear. I had thought it was over with. I had convinced myself that it had never really happened at all. Yet here he is again, demanding that I give him what I have come to detest.

"Please grandpa," I beg, my words muffled against his shirt. The tears are building. I struggle to keep them back.

"Honey it's okay. Grandpa's here to take care of you. Everything's going to be just fine. Oh honey, I love you so much."

He is coaxing me as he pulls me over to the couch. I am tense, my body as rigid as stone. He is pinning me underneath him, balancing himself on top of me while pulling down his pants and then my own. I feel his penis rubbing my leg, making me shudder. He has my right side braced against the couch from shoulder to feet. He is forcing his penis inside me. I am screaming wild tortured sounds which come straight from my soul.

"Jenny baby, just relax. Don't fight me so, just let it feel good. I know how much you like it. Come on girl quit struggling."

His orders are filled with hostility. I lie here eyes shut, wishing he were dead or that I was. His insistent lunging into my body is piercingly painful; his weight oppressively smothering the life out of me. I am pounding on him with clenched fists. He grabs both my hands and holds them together above my head. Forever and ever he bangs away at me. My legs ache and my arms feel as if they are being pulled out of their sockets. He is done, his moans fill the room. He is suffocating me with his bulk. I turn my face refusing to look at him while he croons in my ear.

"Oh Jen, that was so good. I love you baby, don't ever forget it. I missed you so badly. Please honey, don't ever stay away so long again, I need you. I can't take being apart from you like we have been. Remember darling this is our own special secret." His voice is soft and fluid, his breath hot on my cheek.

I don't say a word, I can't. Nothing I feel or say will matter to him. I am still his, he can do with me as he pleases. We both know this is still true. He left soon after, telling me he would see me shortly. I soaked in the bathtub until mama returned four hours later.

Sept. 11, 1963

Dear Diary,

Today was the first day of school. I think sixth grade is going to be much better than any others. I was the only girl in line this morning wearing ankle socks so I went to the bathroom and took them off. Even though I didn't have nylons like most of the others, at least I didn't have to look like a total jerk. I even made a friend today. Her name is Vicki. We decided that from now on we will be best friends and stick up for each other no matter what. I went over to her house and played records. She has the Beatles album that just came out. It's really neat. I think it's going to be fun to have a best friend again.

Oct. 7, 1963

Dear Diary,

I spent the weekend at Vicki's house again. I love being over there even though it's so wild most of the time. Her mom has a new boyfriend that Vicki spies on. She has a crush on him and a boy in our class. Vicki's mom said that in November I can stay the weekend while she goes to Las Vegas. A friend of hers is going to babysit for us. I can't tell mama that her mom won't be home or she won't let me go. Jimmy is coming home in two weeks. David has been paying me to keep his room clean so now I have seventeen dollars saved. I'm going to buy mama a real nice birthday present and a record for Vicki. School is really neat. Vicki and I pretend we are robots and control each other. Mrs. Wilson doesn't like it, but too bad. Yesterday she found the book we are writing about Paula and Paul and she took it away. She's an old biddy.

Vicki was as unhappy with her home life as I was with mine. Although I never told her about Grandpa John it seemed as though she knew that something terrible had happened to me. She was always very gentle with me, never asking more than I was willing to share. We always listened to each others problems and complaints with caring hearts. With Vicki I had finally found a person who liked and accepted me without expecting me to be any different than I already was. From the first day we met we were inseparable. We spent most of our time at her house since her mom was gone so much of the time, and we had all the freedom we wanted. Her mother was divorced and had many boyfriends over to the house. Vicki enjoyed watching her mom and friends kiss and fool around from behind partially closed doors. That was our only difference. While she played detective, I stayed in her bedroom listening to records. Vicki was the most grown up kid I had ever known, surpassing even Sally and Connie. She loved boys and together we would follow whoever she was in love with that week around the neighborhood.

Vicki possessed a lot of information about sex too. When she described the things she saw her mom do I tried to block it out. When that didn't work I pretended to be fascinated with her tales. Vicki wanted to try all the things she had seen. She told me about touching herself and how good it made her feel. Once she even showed me how to do it. I was fascinated and terrified at the same time. She tried to talk me into trying it but when I resisted she gave up her efforts.

Sometimes while spending the night in each other's bed we would pretend to be boyfriend and girlfriends. She was always the boy since she claimed to know about such things. I felt so safe in bed with Vicki. She was warm and soft and always gentle. She was so different than grandpa. I tried not to picture grandpa while she kissed me but sometimes I couldn't make the image of his sagging face disappear and I would start crying right in the middle of her kiss. I never understood exactly why the tears would fall. I only felt embarrassed and ashamed. Vicki just held me tighter and told me she loved me. Other times Vicki would accidentally pin my right arm or leg underneath her causing me to scream out and push her off in a violent rage. Not really knowing what was being triggered within me, I just thought I was crazy. I'm not sure what she thought, she never said. She would just hold me closer and whisper lovingly in my ear. I stayed at Vicki's house as much as our mother's would allow, only going home to mama when necessary. There was nothing at my house for me. There had never been anything but pain waiting there for me.

School was fun because Vicki and I had our own secret world. We didn't let anyone else in. During lunch or recess we went off by ourselves behind the tree to laugh and talk or run after an occasional boy Vicki loved. As time passed and she became less interested in boys, we spent more and more time playing alone. Shortly before Thanksgiving, Vicki's mom went to Las Vegas for the weekend leaving her children with a babysitter. I had permission to spend the time there also. On Sunday the babysitter and her boyfriend took us to the park for a picnic. There were large hills surrounding the park and Vicki, myself and two of her little sisters took off on a mountain climbing expedition soon after we arrived.

After reaching the summit of the mountain we sat down to look at the people below. We had been warned to keep a careful eye out for the younger kids since there were many unexpected ledges and drop offs. Bonnie, Vicki's seven year old sister, was running around throwing pebbles over the side while the rest of us sat giggling and talking. When I thought I saw Bonnie start to fall I ran after her and instead of rescuing her from potential danger I fell over the side of the mountain myself.

The next thing I remember is seeing a blur of faces before me, one of them Vicki's. She was standing, and holding on to herself with tears running down her face. There was a lot of commotion and a searing pain shooting throughout my body. A while later, I was transported to the local hospital in a sheriff's ambulance while Vicki sat beside me holding my hand.

My injuries included a broken arm, fractured ankle and a concussion. It was decided that I should remain in the hospital for a few days of observation. I liked the hospital, the nurses were friendly and kind. The only problem was that Vicki was not allowed to visit with me. I only wanted to go home so that we could be together again. November twenty-second nineteen sixty-three was the day scheduled for my release. Mother arrived at the hospital and took me home around eight the morning of November 22nd, 1963.

"Here's your medicine and some water honey. If the pain gets too bad you can take one of these at ten o'clock. Okay Jen?" Mama seemed very worried about me, I wasn't used to her overt concern, I felt confused by it all.

"Sure mom, I'll be fine, don't worry about me. Just come home as soon as you can, okay?" I felt like I had to take care of her. She looked so frail and tired.

"I'll be home at lunch time, I think you'll be okay until then, don't you?"

"Sure mom, I'm fine. Would you turn on, the TV for me before you leave?"

After turning the set on that had been moved into my room for my convalescence she kissed my cheek and left for work.

I Love Lucy was on first, the episode, where she visits Italy and soaks up the local color by joining some women in the wine making business. Next was Pete and Gladys. While lying there toying with the cast on my arm a news bulletin suddenly interrupted the show.

"President John F. Kennedy has been shot by an unknown assailant while enroute to a speaking engagement in Dallas, Texas just a few minutes ago. He is on his way to Parkland Hospital at this time. We are not sure of his present condition although we so understand he has been seriously wounded."

Is this real? Maybe it's just part of the show, no that doesn't make sense. Can't be real, I just received an autographed picture of him and Jackie and Caroline in the mail last month. Must be some kind of weird joke or something. But no, look, the reporter has tears in his eyes. "I am terribly saddened to announce that the President is dead. I repeat, President John Fitzgerald Kennedy is dead from the bullet of an, unknown assassin. Hearing the front door open I am relieved Mama must have come home early because she heard the new report.

"Mama is that you?" No response. Footsteps on the carpet, softly coming down the hall.

"Hi Jenny, how are you feeling." All smiles, aging blue eyes lit up. "Hey why are you crying? What's going on here?"

Where's mama? "Grandpa, why are you here? Go away, please leave me alone. Didn't you hear? President Kennedy is dead, someone shot him in Dallas this morning. Please go away." Not today, please not today.

"What? Where did you hear that malarkey?"

"Really grandpa, they just said it on TV."

He sits down on the bed, his weight forcing the mattress to sag. Walter Cronkite is talking on the television. I can't watch anymore, all I can see is him here on my bed. Mama please come home now and make him go away. He is just sitting here staring at the man with the grim face on TV. I don't dare take my eyes off of him for a second. I am crying partly for our dead president, but mostly for myself.

Grandpa in my bedroom can only mean one thing. You're an old man, you don't exist. I killed you so many, many times. He doesn't seem to know I am here. If I can only sneak into the bathroom I will be safe. Inching my way slowly, very slowly to the opposite side of the bed where he sits. I must get out of here. My body won't listen, won't do what it must. My legs feel weak and rubbery. My head is playing a game with me. The drums are beating loudly against my temples.

"I don't want to hear this crap!" He is standing up, turning the TV off. No, no. Just go home now, please my body won't move. Please let me get to the bathroom.

"Where are you going little girl?"

Stammering, words won't form on my tongue. "Um uh um I gotta go to the um bathroom."

"Well you just stay there, I'll take you to the toilet later. How's about a back rub? Grandpa feels real sad, I need you to take care of me baby, yea grandpa needs you just like you need him" His eyes, no, not his eyes again, so misty, so full of what he wants. "Come on baby, here honey," reaching over to touch me, "Just let your grandpa roll you over, come on Jenny, just like always." His hands are so large, so cold and transparent. He holds my smaller ones in his, pushing me back into a prone position.

"Grandpa please, I really gotta go bad, okay?" Rambling, trying to distract him, "I can't believe President Kennedy is dead, can you?" Anything, "Wow, why would anyone want to kill him? My mom's coming home soon you know. I sure don't feel good, gotta go to the bathroom real bad too. Hey can you turn the TV on again, I want to see what's going on, okay?"

"Don't worry about anything, grandpa's going to take real good care of you. Now you just lie back there and I'll make you feel real good. You know I was real worried about you when you fell off that cliff. I wouldn't want anything to happen to my little girl now would I?"

Nothing to say, nothing to do, as usual. Grandpa's hands reaching out for me, long snarled fingers pulling on my pajamas. Nearer and nearer. He keeps moving, he's almost on top of me. Tears, go away, don't do me any good anyway. "Please grandpa, please don't touch me. I don't feel good really, please let me sleep awhile grandpa." The sound of my voice is distant and remote as if some other little girl is struggling for her life. His hand is stroking my face, whispers, velvety murmurs of his needs.

"Lovely, lovely Jennifer. Such a beautiful child, grandpa's special girl. Oh, baby, I love you so much." Eyes closed, hurting eyes, shut to keep him out.

"Grandpa, please, please..." Words smothered by heavy parted lips, tongue forcing its way into my mouth.

"Sweet Jenny, my special Jenny, oh baby, what would I do without you?" His whimpering is low and mesmerizing.

"Mama's coming home soon, really grandpa. She's going to come home and make me lunch, please grandpa let me go to the bathroom."

"Jenny why do you lie so much, you and I both know your mother is at work and that's where she's gonna stay. Just you relax honey, grandpa needs you so." Bracing myself against the headboard as he pulls the blankets down around my waist. His fingers unbuttoning my pink pajama top. "Oh Jen, you're so beautiful. Why do you always pretend to not want me. I know you love me as much as I do you, if you'd only cooperate you would feel so good inside." Rough hands, sliding over my chest, nipples pinched between calloused fingers. Tongue leaving trails of saliva down my neck. Mama please come home. Please mama take him away.

"Don't feel good, please, oh God please don't do this anymore." Toes curling around the feet, arms wrapped around my stomach. "Grandpa stop it! Other people don't do this stuff and we're not supposed to either. It's not right!"

"Jenny baby, lots of people love each other like we do. Loving's never wrong, especially when someone loves you as much as I do you. Please just relax, I don't want to have to get mad but you are making me angry."

He is so close now, pinning me up against the back board, his weight crushing me, paralyzing my right side. Struggling wildly, "Get off me, you're killing me."

Wet whispers in my hair,"Baby baby, so good, love you so much." His breathing so heavy, feels hot against my face.

"God I hate you," words coming in gasps, I can't breathe, he is too heavy on me. "Oh God, I hate you."

"Oh baby you shouldn't say such bad things to your grandpa. Don't try to get away, you know you'll never get away from me. You're mine, I'll never let you go."

He sits up, pulling the blankets completely off me. I roll up into a tight little ball and bury my head under the pillows. He is yanking my pants down, I kick and flail aimlessly. His flabby body on top of mine, pressing into my back, squeezing the air out of my lungs. His words droning in my ears, "I love you, you're so good, so warm for me, I know how much you want me, I can feel it." Rolling me over, keeping me down with his massive frame. "Love you, love you, you're mine always, always." His voice, oh God, his voice sending shivers of cold fear down my spine. Sobbing, body wrenching in terror. His hands pinching my breasts, his mouth busily biting my navel.

Now, lying on top of me making it so difficult to breathe, his open mouth buried in my neck, his hands groping, digging into my thighs. The louder I cry and the harder I flail at him with my cast the more he squeezes and bites. Whispers, and low almost pained moaning drowns out my sobs. The sound of his belt buckle being undone, the scratchy noise of his zipper being freed increases the throbbing in my head.

"I hate you! Hate you, you rotten son of a bitch! Get off me, you're hurting me!" Thrashing at him with powerless hands that he doesn't even seem to feel. His hips grinding into mine, soft hardness piercing me. Red, blinding agony from deep within. His knees forcing mine open, stretching them wider, wider still. "No, no, oh God, please no, You're hurting me!" Words choked out in anguished spasms. "Oh Please...no!"

He is driving at me wildly, his body crashing down on mine, pulverizing me into submission. Hopelessly angry screams smothered by bone-crushing lunges, teeth and nails desperately digging into his back. Mama is standing in the doorway, arms braced against each side, her opaque brown eyes gazing into the dark spaces above the bed.

"Mama! Mama!" Arms stretched out above his head, reaching for the shadow propped up in the doorway. "Mama! Help me mommy!" She doesn't, can't see me, her eyes clouded over and far away. "Mama! Oh mama help me..."

Still she stands there, leaning into the wall as if they were one. All the color is drained from her face, her nails gouging into the wood. His head turns to face her, his body leaping up, freeing mine. Someone is howling. Tortured shrieks from a wounded animal pierce the room. Mother's face is all mouth, inhuman sounds coming from her gaping oval. I can't stop moving, jumping, flailing kicking limbs. "Mama, mama!" Grandpa is shaking her, his arms wrapped around her shoulders bouncing her in and out of the door.

"Suzanne, Suzanne! God Damn it Suzanne listen to me!" His hands so abruptly torn from my body are now tearing into hers. "Oh God Suzanne, please listen to me. It isn't what you think, Suzanne!"

Mama is there pushing past him, eyes filled with pain, rushing to the bed of my torment, holding me tightly to her breast. The ominous sound of silence surrounds us. It is just me and mama hanging on to each other, tears flowing together. Clutching me, rocking me back and forth in her warmth. "My baby, my God, Jenny. Jenny, my poor baby, I'm so sorry." Joined by entangled arms we grieve for the loss of our innocence.

Now grandpa stands in the doorway, cigarette dangling from his lips. "Suzanne, I swear it isn't like it seems. She asked me to do it. I swear to you Suzanne, it was all her idea." Rambling lies into mother's iced eyes. "I swear this is the first times you gotta believe me. I wouldn't have done it if she hadn't asked me to. Suzanne, God dammit are you listening to me?" Mama holds me, rocking gently and clinging to the pain. "Suzanne, you gotta hear me, this would kill Sarah, you can't tell your mother, it'll kill her." She doesn't respond, she only holds me tighter. Minutes that felt like hours passed with only the sound of his smoke being blown out through gritted teeth before mama looks me in the eye.

"Honey you gotta take a bath, come on now I'll make you a nice warm tub." Guiding me around the man and down the hall, propping me up with her love. Low groans and teary sobs still beyond my control. I crouch in the corner while she fills the tub. My face is lined with bloody marks of desolation. I can't make my body stop rocking. She lifted me into the tub after delicately removing my remaining clothes and washes me soothingly.

Mama leaves me here to scrub my filth away as I had so many times before after his violence. I try not to listen. but I can't help but hear mama and him talking in the dining room. Mama is screaming and crying like the wounded child I am... I can't really hear their words but the message is clear, he was attempting to coerce her into passivity like he had done to me for the past six years. Grandpa's voice booms throughout the house, blaming me and shouting accusations wherever they might fit in. Then the door slamming. Panic moving deep within my bowels, oh God, did she leave him here with me. Jumping out of the bathtub hurrying to lock the door, ankles giving way, crashing to the tiled floor. Reaching for mother's. razor, I'll kill myself if I hear his voice behind the door. Holding the double edged instrument above my wrist, listening for yet another betrayal. A hand on the doorknob, razor pushed against my bulging vein.

"Jenny, Jenny," mother's voice fluid and wounded. "Jenny why is the door locked? Oh god Jenny, please open the door." Crawling with the razor cupped in my hands, turning the doorknob. Mama rushing in, holding me, holding me as the hysteria mounts and engulfs me.

I don't remember anything else about that day until later that evening. It was around dinner time when the phone rang and mama rushed to answer it. I watched as she spoke softly into the receiver crying all the while. I was very confused and afraid. I didn't know what was taking place but I had a gut feeling it was about me. She finally finished the phone conversation and returned to her dinner. She appeared on the verge of collapse as he hung her head on the table and wept into her arms.

After many minutes of my brother and sister and I silently staring at her she spoke softly. "Your grandfather has turned himself into the police. He is in a mental hospital." Her words were barely audible as she continued. "He has hurt Jenny very badly. He is a very sick man and needs to be taken care of by people who know how to deal with this type of thing."

Debbie and David stared open mouthed at me. I interpreted their looks as anger and blame.

"What are you talking about mom? What happened?, Debbie asked.

"Grandpa touched her in a sexual way, That's all there is to say about it. He's a very sick man, it wasn't his fault. You mustn't be upset with him, he couldn't help it. He'll get help and he'll be fine."

They both turned to me as if expecting me to add something. I was speechless. How could she say it wasn't his fault? Did that mean it really was my fault as I had thought? Did she hate me? Did they all hate me? Would they lock me up in a place for crazy people too? What would happen to my Grandma Sarah? Who would take care of her? What had I done now? Why were they glaring at me as if I were the bad one? Why weren't they mad at grandpa for hurting me? I was to blame for my mother's crying and feeling hurt. It was my fault grandpa was locked up in a nut house. My guilt only intensified as mother's weeping escalated, and she ran into her room.

I do not remember any more of the details of the night that was the turning point in my life. I only recall the fear and tremendous guilt I experienced at the time. The nearly seven years of torture I endured under Grandpa John were not to be discussed again. My suffering would for many years remain the family secret and shame.

EPILOGUE

There comes a time when you can no longer hang on by a shred of lost hope to the tightrope that threatens to break. A moment so still that all you can hear is the grating sound of the rope as it pulls away, ever so slowly, from the source of its strength. A time when all you are really sure of is how the rhythm of your heart resembles the beating of ancient drums as a human sacrifice is placed on the altar of your nightmares. A split second when no matter how deeply you breathe, the oxygen refuses to fill your lungs and you are sure you are suffocating. For a fleeting moment there is nothing else except for the shadowy glimpse of a faded negative from too many years ago and a sudden realization that you no longer know what the battle is all about. At this very instant, and no other, you must choose to either let go and breathe freely again or stay and fester in the infection that has become your life.

We all have some secret from our past that we keep hidden in the deepest recesses of our being. Something that we clutch onto so tightly that its life is smothered into formless ashes brushed into a heap in some far away corner. With our individual badges of guilt and suffering we are made unique in a jungle of imitations and look alikes. Our secrets explain and identify us for the world. Some of us hold on longer and harder because there is nothing else that separates us from the faceless crowd. Some of us, grudgingly, let go, at least some of the way, and mingle with the nameless in the blur of our existence. Still others go down sinking into the depths of black murk in order not to give up what keeps them alive.

Our differences pull us apart and draw us together like magnets of indestructible steel. Our sameness is denied through distortions of our uniqueness. We search for the minute link, some slender, fragile thread that binds our souls as one. Yet still we grasp onto the pain that alienates and protects us from the intimacy we believe we want. We wrap our pain around ourselves with pride.

Not many of us ever really stop to think about this; we go about our lives as though walking through a maze that we have little inclination to abandon. It seems somewhat of a miracle that a few of us are able to fight and claw our way out of the trenches to discover a sun that lights our way.

For twenty-eight years I kept my aloneness and shame buried in layers of rot and stench that oozed from my wounds of hatred. The blistering scab served as a lone warrior's shield against intimacy, true connection and love. No, the choice was not an obvious one, the decision not premeditated. The anguish of too many lonely, desperate nights filled with undefinable terror, or perhaps, too many pills devoured in solitude had forced the choice into an eruption no longer able to be disguised or denied.

Looking back, it seems that someone else made the decision for me, someone whose realness touched mine, though now I know that wasn't really so. I did this painfully alone, as we all must. Until just recently I didn't even know that the choice to integrate the abandoned child within me had been decided at such a clear and precise moment.

The room is small and cluttered with remnants of her caring. Ghosts of other sorrows can be felt in the smoke stale air. The worn chairs hold the imprint of all that have sought solace from the tiny woman who now fills the room with acceptance and love. My self portrait hangs on the wall, sneering down at me, between happier scenes of the way life is 'supposed' to be. I stand, blending into the textured wall, pretending to be fascinated by the cars parked in the lot below my window view. She sits there, quietly smoking a cigarette, her legs propped up on a rattan stool. I watch her every move from the corner of my clouded eyes. Such a small person to be so big. I catch her watching me and turn my head in shame. Kicking the wall I notice other foot smudges from other frustrations. The silence is so deafening I want to scream. I bury my head in the corner, feeling the cold sterility of the window pane on one cheek and the warm cotton of my blouse on the other. I wait, impatiently, for her to say something, anything. She sits there rubbing the back of her calves with one hand and blowing too blue smoke through slightly parted lips, as if on the verge of some long anticipated declaration. Still she utters not a sound. She sees me through eyes that have only recently learned to love. Her caring seems to hang in the air, hovering above me, before coming to rest on my slouching shoulders. I feel the demand the depth of her loving requires. I try to shake it off, avoid the bonding, by kicking her chair, as if to knock her off the pedestal I have created. I know she wishes she could reach me. I believe she wants to hold me to her breasts as if I really were the innocent child we are working so hard to discover.

I pace the room, counting each step it takes to avoid her unconditional affection. Hearing the low creaking of her rocking chair I turn to confront eyes that know too much about where I have been and who I am becoming. I see soft brown eyes framed by large glasses that are too small to conceal her warmth. If only her eyes were blue I could leave her with the bitter victory of hatred on my side. Damn her anyway! Why does she delay so torturously what I know she must demand. Love always demands payment, one way or another. I am convinced I must bide my time, if I wait long enough she will ask that I do the unspeakable. Then I can leave her, despise her rightfully; be able to fit her into the only reality I have ever known. Then she will be, as she surely must, like all the others who have spoken of love in one breath and struck out with rage and hatred the next.

Still she utters not a word. I listen closely for the sound of her breathing as I hesitate in my journey away from myself. I sit, rock violently, glare at her, my eyes too full to veil the need of her. I lean back, head against rough orange cloth. I spy a spot on the ceiling where it once must have leaked with rain; I fight to stay in the now, the struggle to escape to the ceiling's safety so strong. The clock on the desk must be broken, its hands appear permanently stuck at four seventeen.

I see my reflection in the side of a chipped cup tenderly filled with almond tea. Staring back at me is an ageless child. Her green eyes are large and haunting; they pierce though me leaving me chilled and empty. Her hair is blown free and in a tangled mess seems to silhouette her face like the ones of George Washington she made in the first grade. I think, I fear that I recognize the girl in the tea cup. She reminds me of someone I vaguely knew, once, many years ago.

Still the woman in the chair, with her feet up, says nothing. I fumble in my purse for a cigarette, my hands tripping over each other. The high pitched whining of voiceless sounds seem to fill the room beyond capacity. At any moment I expect the walls to explode outwardly.

The skinned kneed, brown haired six year old hides behind my hair, fighting for her freedom. Her cat-like green eyes beg for my compassion. Her chewed-down-to-the quick fingernails claw, at my face leaving trails of fresh blood to remind me of her dominance. The woman leans towards me, her elbow resting on the desk supporting the palm that cups her chin. She seems to be saying something I cannot hear. Her mouth moves, with mimicking words that have no substance. The oval of her lips appears to be mouthing the word yes, yes over and over again.

The little girl with the invisible scars grows bigger in the tea cup. I watch with open mouthed fascination as she approaches me. Her spindly arms reach out for me. I tremble as tears flow down my cheeks. For the first time ever I see that she is a beautiful child; not the dirty ugly girl I believed her to be.

The woman next to me now, still mouthing inaudible sounds. As she reaches out her hand to guide me as I hesitantly reach out mine and span the twenty-four years of separateness. I weep as I embrace the sad eyed little girl child within me and become one.